Low Carb High Fat Diet

Second edition

By Don Orwell

http://SuperfoodsToday.com

Disclaimer:

The Information presented in this book is created to provide useful information on the subject areas discussed. The publisher and author are not accountable for any particular health or allergic reaction needs that may involve medical supervision and are not liable for any damage or damaging outcomes from any treatment, application or preparation, action, to any person reading or adhering to the information in this book. References are presented for informational reasons only and do not represent an endorsement of any web sites or other sources. Audience should be informed that the websites mentioned in this book may change.

This publication includes opinions and ideas of its author and is meant for informational purposes only. The author and publisher shall in no event be held liable for any damage or loss sustained from the usage of this publication.

Your Free Gift

As a way of saying thanks for your purchase, I'm offering you my FREE eBook that is exclusive to my book and blog readers.

Superfoods Cookbook - Book Two has over 70 Superfoods recipes and complements Superfoods Cookbook Book One and it contains Superfoods Salads, Superfoods Smoothies and Superfoods Deserts with ultra-healthy non-refined ingredients. All ingredients are 100% Superfoods.

It also contains Superfoods Reference book which is organized by Superfoods (more than 60 of them, with the list of their benefits), Superfoods spices, all vitamins, minerals and antioxidants. Superfoods Reference Book lists Superfoods that can help with 12 diseases and 9 types of cancer.

http://www.SuperfoodsToday.com/FREE

Table of Contents

Introduction

Hello,

My name is Don Orwell and my blog SuperfoodsToday.com is dedicated to Superfoods Lifestyle.

This book contains Superfoods Low Carb High Fat recipes from my other books. I hope that you will enjoy 100% Superfoods recipes that I prepared for you.

Superfoods Low Carb High Fat Recipes

Allergy labels: SF – Soy Free, GF – Gluten Free, DF – Dairy Free, EF – Egg Free, V - Vegan, NF – Nut Free

Condiments

Basil Pesto

- 1 cup basil
- 1/3 cup cashews
- 2 garlic cloves, chopped
- 1/2 cup olive oil

Process basil, cashews and garlic until smooth. Add oil in a slow stream. Process to combine. Transfer to a bowl. Season with salt and pepper. Stir to combine. Allergies: SF, GF, DF, EF, V

Cilantro Pesto

- 1 cup cilantro
- 1/3 cup cashews
- 2 garlic cloves, chopped
- 1/2 cup olive oil or avocado oil

Process cilantro, cashews and garlic. Add oil in a slow stream. Process to combine. Transfer to a bowl. Season with salt and pepper. Stir to combine. Allergies: SF, GF, DF, EF, V

Sundried Tomato Pesto

- 3/4 cup sundried tomatoes
- 1/3 cup cashews
- 2 garlic cloves, chopped
- 1/2 cup olive oil or avocado oil

Process tomato, cashews and garlic. Add oil in a slow stream. Process to combine. Transfer to a bowl. Season with salt and pepper. Stir to combine. Allergies: SF, GF, DF, EF, V

Savory Breakfasts

Serves 1

Regular egg recipes

Allergies: SF, GF, DF, NF

Eggs are great way to start a day and you can enjoy them hard boiled, scrambled, poached or in the omelet with veggies. Eat some breakfast veggies with eggs.

Omelet with Leeks

Serves 1 - Allergies: SF, GF, DF, NF

Cook leeks in little coconut oil until they get soft and then mix the beaten eggs in.

Egg pizza crust

Ingredients - Allergies: SF, GF, DF, NF

- 3 eggs
- 1/2 cup of coconut flour
- 1 cup of coconut milk
- 1 crushed garlic clove

Mix and make an omelet.

Omelet with Superfoods veggies

Serves 1

Ingredients - Allergies: SF, GF, DF, NF

- 2 large eggs
- Salt
- Ground black pepper
- 1 tsp. olive oil or cumin oil
- 1 cup spinach, cherry tomatoes and 1 spoon of yogurt cheese
- Crushed red pepper flakes and a pinch of dill (optional)

Instructions

Whisk 2 large eggs in a small bowl. Season with salt and ground black pepper and set aside. Heat 1 tsp. olive oil in a medium skillet over medium heat. Add baby spinach, tomatoes, cheese and cook, tossing, until wilted (Approx. 1 minute). Add eggs; cook, stirring occasionally, until just set, about 1 minute. Stir in cheese. Sprinkle with crushed red pepper flakes and dill.

Egg Muffins

Ingredients - Allergies: SF, GF, DF, NF

Serving: 8 muffins

- 8 eggs
- 1 cup diced green bell pepper
- 1 cup diced onion
- 1 cup spinach
- 1/4 tsp. salt
- 1/8 tsp. ground black pepper
- 2 tbsp. water

Instructions

Heat the oven to 350 degrees F. Oil 8 muffin cups. Beat eggs together. Mix in bell pepper, spinach, onion, salt, black pepper, and water. Pour that mixture in the muffin cups. Bake in the oven until muffins are done in the middle.

Smoked Salmon Scrambled Eggs

Ingredients, serves 2 - Allergies: SF, GF, DF, NF

- 1 tsp coconut oil
- 4 eggs
- 1 Tbs water
- 4 oz smoked salmon, sliced
- 1/2 avocado
- ground black pepper, to taste
- 4 chives, minced (or use 1 green onion, thinly sliced)

Instructions

Heat a skillet over medium heat. Add coconut oil to pan when hot. Meanwhile, scramble eggs. Add eggs to the hot skillet, along with smoked salmon. Stirring continuously, cook eggs until soft and fluffy.

Remove from heat. Top with avocado, black pepper, and chives to serve.

Steak and Eggs

Serves 2

Ingredients - Allergies: SF, GF, DF, NF

- 1/2 lb boneless beef steak or pork tenderloin
- 1/4 tsp ground black pepper
- 1/4 tsp sea salt (optional)
- 2 tsp coconut oil
- 1/4 onion, diced
- 1 red bell pepper, diced
- 1 handful spinach or arugula
- 2 eggs

Instructions

Season sliced steak or pork tenderloin with sea salt and black pepper. Heat a sauté pan over high heat. Add 1 tsp coconut oil, onions, and meat when pan is hot, and sauté until steak is slightly cooked. Add spinach and red bell pepper, and cook until steak is done to your liking. Meanwhile, heat a small fry pan over medium heat. Add remaining coconut oil, and fry two eggs. Top each steak with a fried egg to serve.

Egg Bake

Ingredients - Allergies: SF, GF, DF, NF

Serves 6

- 2 cups chopped red peppers or spinach
- 1 cup zucchini
- 2 tbsp. coconut oil
- 1 cup sliced mushrooms
- 1/2 cup sliced green onions
- 8 eggs
- 1 cup coconut milk
- 1/2 cup almond flour
- 2 tbsp. minced fresh parsley
- 1/2 tsp. dried basil
- 1/2 tsp. salt
- 1/4 tsp. ground black pepper

Instructions

Preheat oven to 350 degrees F. Put coconut oil in a skillet. Heat it to medium heat. Add mushrooms, onions, zucchini and red pepper (or spinach) until vegetables are tender, about 5 minutes. Drain veggies and spread them over the baking dish.

Beat eggs in a bowl with milk, flour, parsley, basil, salt, and pepper. Pour egg mixture into baking dish.

Bake in preheated oven until the center is set (approx. 35 to 40 minutes).

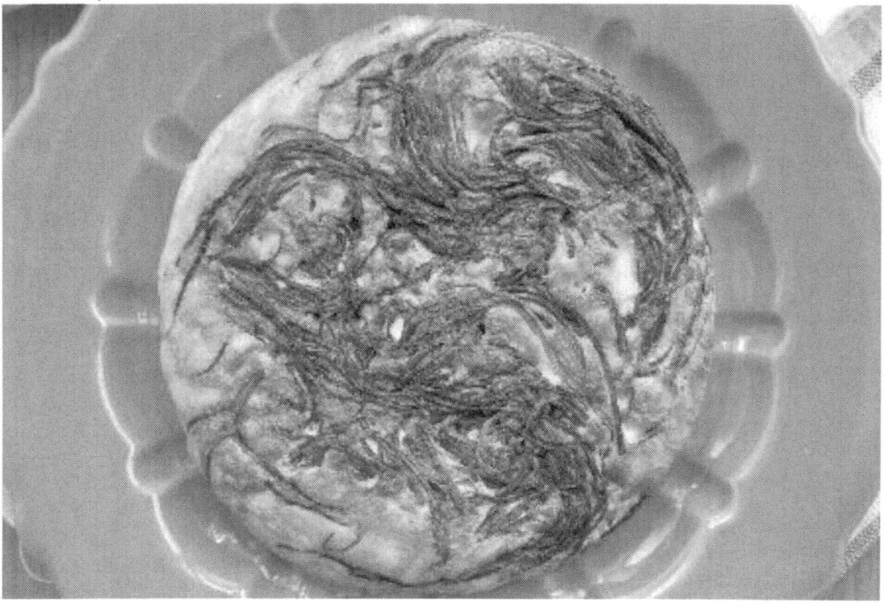

Frittata

6 servings

Ingredients - Allergies: SF, GF, DF, NF

- 2 tbsp. olive oil or avocado oil
- 1 Zucchini, sliced
- 1 cup torn fresh spinach
- 2 tbsp. sliced green onions
- 1 tsp. crushed garlic, salt and pepper to taste
- 1/3 cup coconut milk
- 6 eggs

Instructions

Heat olive oil in a skillet over medium heat. Add zucchini and cook until tender. Mix in spinach, green onions, and garlic. Season with salt and pepper. Continue cooking until spinach is wilted.

In a separate bowl, beat together eggs and coconut milk. Pour into the skillet over the vegetables. Reduce heat to low, cover, and cook until eggs are firm (5 to 7 minutes).

Zucchini Pancakes

Serves 3

Ingredients - Allergies: SF, GF, DF

- 2 medium zucchini
- 2 tbsp. chopped onion
- 3 beaten eggs
- 6 to 8 tbsp. almond flour
- 1 tsp. salt
- 1/2 tsp. ground black pepper
- coconut oil

Instructions

Heat the oven to 300 degrees F.

Grate the zucchini into a bowl and stir in the onion and eggs. Stir in 6 tbsp. of the flour, salt, and pepper.

Heat a large sauté pan over medium heat and add coconut oil in the pan. When the oil is hot, lower the heat to medium-low and add batter into the pan. Cook the pancakes about 2 minutes on each side, until browned. Place the pancakes in the oven.

Cottage Cheese Sesame Balls

Ingredients - Allergies: SF, GF, EF

- 16 ounce farmers cheese or cottage cheese
- 1 cup finely chopped almonds
- 1and 1/2 cups oatmeal

In a large bowl, combine blended cottage cheese, almonds and oatmeal. Make balls and roll in sesame seeds mix.

Frittata with Carrots, Green Peas and Asparagus

Serves 1

Ingredients - Allergies: SF, GF, DF, NF

- 2 large eggs
- Salt
- Ground black pepper
- 1 tsp. olive oil or avocado oil
- 1/2 cup cooked green peas
- 1/2 cup chopped carrot
- 1/2 cup asparagus
- 1 tbsp. fresh dill

Instructions

Whisk 2 large eggs in a small bowl. Season with salt and ground black pepper and set aside. Heat 1 tsp. oil in a medium skillet over medium heat. Add carrots and asparagus and cook, tossing, approx. 5 minutes. Add cooked and drained green peas. Add eggs; cook, stirring occasionally, until just set, about 1 minute. Sprinkle with dill.

Frittata with Asparagus and Tomato

Serves 1

Ingredients - Allergies: SF, GF, DF, NF

- 2 large eggs
- Salt
- Ground black pepper
- 1 tsp. olive oil or avocado oil
- 1 cup asparagus
- 1/2 cup sliced tomatoes

Instructions

Whisk 2 large eggs in a small bowl. Season with salt and ground black pepper and set aside. Heat 1 tsp. oil in a medium skillet over medium heat. Add asparagus and cook, tossing approx. 4-5 minutes. Add tomatoes and eggs and cook, stirring occasionally, until just set, about 1 minute. Sprinkle with dill (optional).

Leeks, Spinach, Eggs & Yogurt

Serves 1

Ingredients - Allergies: SF, GF, DF, NF

- 2 large eggs
- Salt
- Ground black pepper
- 1 tsp. olive oil or avocado oil
- 1/2 cup sliced leeks
- 1/3 cup spinach
- 1/3 cup thick Greek yogurt

Instructions

Heat 1 tsp. olive oil in a medium skillet over medium heat. Add leeks and coook for 5 minutes. Add spinach, salt and pepper and cook, tossing, until wilted (Approx. 1 minute). Break eggs on top and fry until done. Top with yogurt.

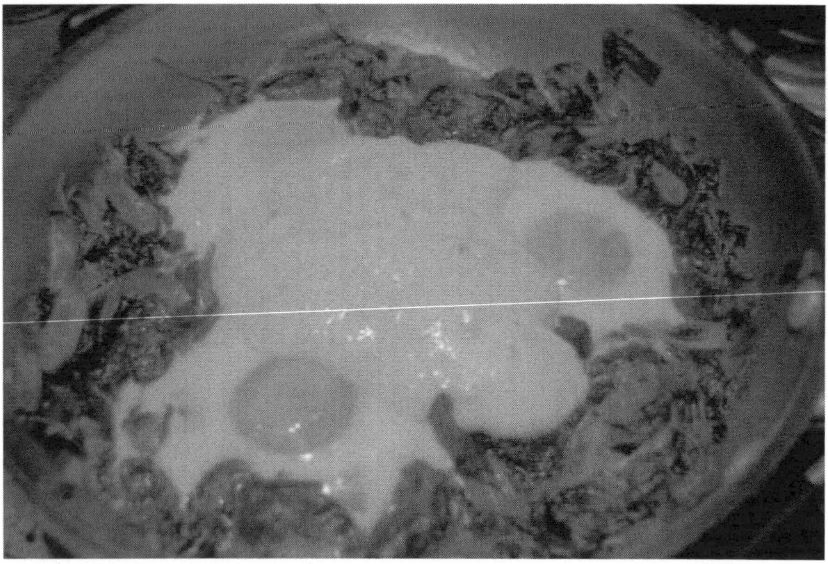

Broccoli Frittata

Serves 1

Ingredients - Allergies: SF, GF, DF, NF

- 2 large eggs
- Salt
- Ground black pepper
- 1 tsp. olive oil or avocado oil
- 1 cup Broccoli

Instructions

Whisk 2 large eggs in a small bowl. Season with salt and ground black pepper and set aside. Heat 1 tsp. olive oil in a medium skillet over medium heat. Add broccoli and cook, tossing, approx. 4-5 minutes. Add eggs; cook, stirring occasionally, until just set.

Mushrooms Omelet

Ingredients - Allergies: SF, GF, DF, NF

- 2 large eggs
- Salt
- Ground black pepper
- 1 tsp. olive oil or avocado oil
- 1 cup mushrooms

Instructions

Whisk 2 large eggs in a small bowl. Season with salt and ground black pepper and set aside. Heat 1 tsp. olive oil in a medium skillet over medium heat. Add mushrooms and cook, tossing, until slightly wilted (Approx. 3 minutes). Set aside. Add eggs and cook until set. Add mushrooms on top of the eggs. Flip eggs over mushrooms.

Broccoli, Red Peppers &Mushrooms Omelet

Ingredients - Allergies: SF, GF, DF, NF

- 2 large eggs
- Salt
- Ground black pepper
- 1 tsp. olive oil or avocado oil
- 1/2 cup broccoli
- 1/2 cup red peppers and mushrooms

Instructions

Whisk 2 large eggs in a small bowl. Season with salt and ground black pepper and set aside. Heat 1 tsp. olive oil in a medium skillet over medium heat. Add all veggies and cook, tossing, until slightly wilted (Approx. 3 minutes). Set aside. Add eggs and cook until set. Add veggies on top of the eggs. Flip eggs over veggies.

Broths

Some recipes require a cup or more of various broths, vegetable, beef or chicken broth. I usually cook the whole pot and freeze it in one cup or half a cup chunks.

Vegetable broth

Servings: 6 cups

Ingredients

- 1 tbsp. coconut oil
- 1 large onion, chopped
- 2 stalks celery, including some leaves
- 2 large carrots, chopped
- 1 bunch green onions, chopped
- 8 cloves garlic, minced
- 8 sprigs fresh parsley
- 6 sprigs fresh thyme
- 2 bay leaves
- 1 tsp. salt
- 2 quarts water

Instructions - Allergies: SF, GF, DF, EF, V, NF

Put all ingredients in slow cooker and cook on low for 4 hours. Other ingredients to consider: broccoli stalk, celery root. Let cool to warm room temperature and strain. Keep chilled and use or freeze broth within a few days.

Chicken Broth

Ingredients

- 4 lbs. fresh chicken (wings, necks, backs, legs, bones)
- 2 peeled onions or 1 cup chopped leeks
- 2 celery stalks
- 1 carrot
- 8 black peppercorns
- 2 sprigs fresh thyme
- 2 sprigs fresh parsley
- 1 tsp. salt

Instructions - Allergies: SF, GF, DF, EF, NF

Put all ingredients in slow cooker and cook on low for 6 hours. Let cool to warm room temperature and strain. Keep chilled and use or freeze broth within a few days.

Beef Broth

Ingredients

- 4-5 pounds beef bones and few veal bones
- 1 pound of stew meat (chuck or flank steak) cut into 2-inch chunks
- Olive oil
- 1-2 medium onions, peeled and quartered
- 1-2 large carrots, cut into 1-2 inch segments
- 1 celery rib, cut into 1 inch segments
- 2-3 cloves of garlic, unpeeled
- Handful of parsley, stems and leaves
- 1-2 bay leaves
- 10 peppercorns

Instructions - Allergies: SF, GF, DF, EF, NF

Heat oven to 375°F. Rub olive oil over the stew meat pieces, carrots, and onions. Place stew meat or beef scraps, stock bones, carrots and onions in a large roasting pan. Roast in oven for about 45 minutes, turning everything half-way through the cooking.

Place everything from the oven in the slow cooker and cook on low for 6 hours. After cooking, remove the bones and vegetables from the pot. Strain the broth. Let cool to room temperature and then put in the refrigerator.

The fat will solidify once the broth has chilled. Discard the fat (or reuse it) and pour the broth into a jar and freeze it.

Tomato paste

Some recipes (chili) require tomato paste. I usually prepare 20 or so liters at once (when tomato is in season, which is usually September) and freeze it.

Ingredients

- 5 lbs. chopped plum tomatoes
- 1/4 cup extra-virgin olive oil plus 2 tbsp.
- salt, to taste

Instructions - Allergies: SF, GF, DF, EF, V, NF

Heat 1/4 cup of the oil in a skillet over medium heat. Add tomatoes. Season with salt. Bring to a boil. Cook, stirring, until very soft, about 8 minutes.

Pass the tomatoes through the finest plate of a food mill. Push as much of the pulp through the sieve as possible and leave the seeds behind.

Cook in slow cooker for 4 hours on low.
Store sealed in an airtight container in the refrigerator for up to one month, or freeze, for up to 6 months.

Curry Paste

This can be prepared in advance and frozen. There are several curry recipes that are using curry paste and I decided to take the curry paste recipe out and have it separately. So, when you see that the recipe is using curry paste, please go to this part of the book and prepare it from scratch or defrost of you have it frozen. Don't use processed curry pastes or curry powder; make it every time from scratch. Keep the spices in original form (seeds, pods), ground them just before making the curry paste. You can dry heat in the skillet cloves, cardamom, cumin and coriander and then crush them coarsely with mortar and pestle.

Ingredients

- 2 onions, minced
- 2 cloves garlic, minced
- 2 teaspoons fresh ginger root, finely chopped
- 6 whole cloves
- 2 cardamom pods
- 2 (2 inch) pieces cinnamon sticks, crushed
- 1 tsp. ground cumin
- 1 tsp. ground coriander
- 1 tsp. salt
- 1 tsp. ground cayenne pepper
- 1 tsp. ground turmeric

Instructions - Allergies: SF, GF, DF, EF, V, NF

Heat oil in a frying pan over medium heat and fry onions until transparent. Stir in garlic, cumin, ginger, cloves, cinnamon, coriander, salt, cayenne, and turmeric. Cook for 1 minute over medium heat, stirring constantly. At this point other curry ingredients should be added or let cook and freeze.

Healthy Superfoods Casserole Sauce

- 2 beaten eggs
- Salt, pepper
- 1 cup of low-fat Greek yogurt
- 1 Tbsp. olive oil
- 1/2 cup of low fat parmesan or shredded cheddar cheese

Optional:

- 1 tsp of flax seeds meal
- 1/2 tsp. oregano or thyme or any other herbs

Precooked beans

Again, some recipes require that you cook some beans (low carb ones, cannellini beans, mung beans, black beans) in advance. Cooking beans takes around 3 hours and it can be done in advance or every few weeks and the rest get frozen. Soak beans for 24 hours before cooking them. After the first boil, throw the water, add new water and continue cooking. Some beans or lentils can be sprouted for few days before cooking and that helps if you have stomach problems.

Soups

Lentil Soup

Serves 4-6

Ingredients - Allergies: SF, GF, DF, EF, NF

- 2 tbsp. olive oil or avocado oil
- 1 cup finely chopped onion
- 1/2 cup chopped carrot
- 1/2 cup chopped celery
- 2 teaspoons salt
- 1 pound lentils
- 1 cup chopped tomatoes
- 2 quarts chicken or vegetable broth
- 1/2 tsp. ground coriander & toasted cumin

Instructions

Put all ingredients in the slow cooker and cook on low for 4 hours.

Bouillabaisse

Serves 6.

Ingredients - Allergies: SF, GF, DF, EF, NF

- 3 pounds of 3 different kinds of fish fillets
- 1/2 cup coconut oil
- 1-2 pounds of Oysters, clams, or mussels
- 1 cup cooked shrimp, crab, or lobster meat, or rock lobster tails
- 1 cup thinly sliced onions
- 4 Shallots or the white parts of 2 or 3 leeks, thinly sliced
- 2 cloves garlic, crushed
- 1 large tomato, chopped
- 1 sweet red pepper, chopped
- 4 stalks celery, thinly sliced
- 2-inch slice of fennel or 1 tsp. of fennel seed
- 3 sprigs fresh thyme or 3/4 tsp. dried thyme
- 1 bay leaf
- 2-3 whole cloves
- Zest of half an orange
- 1/2 tsp. saffron
- 2 teaspoons salt
- 1/4 tsp. ground black pepper
- 1 cup clam juice or fish broth
- 2 Tbps lemon juice
- 2/3 cup white wine

Instructions

Put all ingredients in the slow cooker and cook on low for 4 hours.

Italian Beef Soup

Serves 6

Ingredients - Allergies: SF, GF, DF, EF, NF

- 1 pound minced beef
- 1 clove garlic, minced
- 4 cups beef broth
- 1 tomato
- 1/2 cup sliced carrots
- 2 cups raw beans
- 2 small zucchini, cubed
- 2 cups spinach - rinsed and torn
- 1/4 tsp. black pepper
- 1/4 tsp. salt

Put all ingredients in slow cooker and cook on low for 8 hours.

Black Bean Soup

Serves 6-8

Ingredients - Allergies: SF, GF, DF, EF, NF

- 1/4 cup coconut oil
- 1 cup Onions, Diced
- 1 cup Carrots, Diced
- 1 cup Green Bell Pepper, Diced
- 3 cup beef broth
- 2 cups raw Black Beans
- 1 tbsp. lemon juice
- 2 teaspoons Garlic
- 2 teaspoons Salt
- 1/2 tsp. Black Pepper, Ground
- 2 teaspoons Chili Powder
- 1 pound cubed pork
- 1 tbsp. tapioca flour
- 2 cups Water

Instructions

Put all ingredients in slow cooker and cook on low for 8 hours.

Squash soup

Serves 4-6

Ingredients - Allergies: SF, GF, DF, EF, V, NF

- 1 Squash, skin and seeds removed, chopped
- 1 carrot, chopped
- 1 onion (diced)
- 3/4 – 1 cup coconut milk
- 1 cup water
- olive oil or avocado oil
- Salt
- Pepper
- Cinnamon
- Turmeric

Instructions

Put all ingredients in the slow cooker and cook on low for 4 hours. Blend until smooth and creamy. Sprinkle it with toasted pumpkin seeds.

Kale Cannellini Beans Pork Soup

Serves 4-6

Ingredients - Allergies: SF, GF, DF, EF, NF

- 2 tbsp. each extra-virgin olive oil or cumin oil and coconut oil
- 3 tbsp. chili powder
- 1 tbsp. jalapeno hot sauce
- 2 pounds bone-in pork chops
- Salt
- 4 stalks celery, chopped
- 1 large white onion, chopped
- 3 cloves garlic, chopped
- 3 cups chicken broth
- 1/2 cup diced tomatoes
- 2 cups raw cannellini beans
- 6 cups packed Kale

Instructions

Put all ingredients in the slow cooker and cook for 8 hours on low.

Avgolemono – Greek lemon chicken soup

Serves 4

Ingredients - Allergies: SF, GF, DF, EF, NF

- 4 cups chicken broth
- 1/4 cup uncooked quinoa
- salt and pepper
- 3 eggs
- 3 tbsp. lemon juice
- Handful fresh dill (chopped)
- shredded roasted chicken (optional)

Whisk lemon juice and the eggs until smooth. Add about 1 cup of the hot broth into the egg/lemon mixture and whisk to combine.

Put all ingredients in the slow cooker and cook on low for 4 hours.

Minestrone

Serves 8-10

Ingredients - Allergies: SF, GF, DF, EF, NF

- 3 tbsp. coconut oil
- 3 cloves garlic, chopped
- 2 onions, chopped
- 2 cups chopped celery
- 2 carrots, sliced
- 2 cups chicken broth
- 2 cups water
- 1 cup tomato sauce
- 1/2 oz. red wine (optional)
- 1 cup raw cannellini beans
- 2 cups green beans
- 2 cups baby spinach, rinsed
- 3 zucchinis, quartered and sliced
- 1 tbsp. chopped oregano
- 2 tbsp. chopped basil
- salt and pepper to taste
- 1 tbsp. olive oil or cumin oil

Instructions

Put all ingredients in the slow cooker and cook on low for 6 hours.

Cioppino

Serves 6

Ingredients - Allergies: SF, GF, DF, EF, NF

- 3/4 cup coconut oil
- 2 onions, chopped
- 2 cloves garlic, minced
- 1 bunch fresh parsley, chopped
- 1,5 cups stewed tomatoes
- 1,5 cups chicken broth
- 2 bay leaves
- 1 tbsp. dried basil
- 1/2 tsp. dried thyme
- 1/2 tsp. dried oregano
- 1 cup water
- 1-1/2 cups white wine
- 1-1/2 pounds peeled and deveined large shrimp
- 1-1/2 pounds bay scallops
- 18 small clams
- 18 cleaned and debearded mussels
- 1-1/2 cups crabmeat
- 1-1/2 pounds cod fillets, cubed

Instructions

Put all ingredients in the slow cooker and cook on low for 4 hours.

Bean Soup

Serves 6

Ingredients - Allergies: SF, GF, DF, EF, NF

- 2 cups beef broth
- 4 cups water
- 2 cups sliced carrots
- 2 cups raw white beans
- 1 cup sliced celery & 1 cup sliced leeks
- 2 cups sliced onions
- 1/4 tsp. black pepper
- 1 clove garlic, minced, 1 Tbsp. minced ginger, 3 bay leaves
- 1/2 tsp. salt
- 1 pound minced pork

Put all ingredients in slow cooker and cook on low for 8 hours.

Chicken Winter Soup

Serves 6

Ingredients - Allergies: SF, GF, DF, EF, NF

- 2 pounds chicken pieces with skin on
- 1 clove garlic, minced, 1 Tbsp. minced ginger, 3 bay leaves
- 6 cups water
- ½ cup sliced parsley & ½ cup sliced cilantro
- 2 cups sliced carrots
- 1 cup sliced celery
- 1 cup sliced spring onions
- 2 cups sliced onions
- 1/4 tsp. black pepper
- 1/4 tsp. salt

Put all ingredients in slow cooker and cook on low for 8 hours.

Pot Roast Soup

Serves 6

Ingredients - Allergies: SF, GF, DF, EF, NF

- 1 pound leftover pot roast
- 1 clove garlic, minced, 1 Tbsp. minced ginger
- 5 cups beef broth
- 2 sliced tomatoes
- 1 cup julienned carrots
- 2 cups julienned zucchini
- 1 cup green peas
- 1/4 cups chopped parsley
- 1 cup sliced onions
- 1/4 tsp. black pepper
- 1/4 tsp. salt

Put all ingredients in slow cooker and cook on low for 8 hours.

Minced Pork & Tomato Soup

Serves 6

Ingredients - Allergies: SF, GF, DF, EF, NF

- 1 pound minced pork
- 1 clove garlic, minced, 1 Tbsp. minced ginger, 3 bay leaves
- 2 cups water
- 2 cups tomato paste
- 3 cups beef broth
- ½ cup sliced parsley
- 2 cups sliced carrots
- 1 cup sliced celery
- 1/2 cups corn and & ½ cups sliced yellow pepper
- 1 cup sliced green beans
- 2 cups sliced onions
- 1/4 tsp. black pepper
- 1/4 tsp. salt

Put all ingredients in slow cooker and cook on low for 8 hours.

Tomato, Star Anise, Chicken & Leeks Soup

Serves 6

Ingredients - Allergies: SF, GF, DF, EF, NF

- 3 cups chicken broth
- 2 cups water
- 2 cups sliced tomatoes
- 3 cups sliced leeks
- 1 cup sliced celery
- 1 pound chicken
- 1/4 tsp. black pepper
- 4 star anise
- 1 clove garlic, minced, 1 Tbsp. minced ginger, 3 bay leaves
- 1/2 tsp. salt

Put all ingredients in slow cooker and cook on low for 8 hours.

Salads

Greek Cucumber Salad

Serves 2-3

Ingredients - Allergies: SF, GF, EF, NF

- 2-3 cucumbers, sliced
- 2 teaspoons salt
- 3 tbsp. lemon juice
- 1/4 tsp. paprika
- 1/4 tsp. white pepper
- 1/2 clove garlic, minced
- 4 fresh green onions, diced
- 1 cup thick Greek Yogurt
- 1/4 tsp. paprika

Instructions

Slice cucumbers thinly, sprinkle with salt and mix. Set aside for one hour. Mix lemon juice, water, garlic, paprika and white pepper, and set aside. Squeeze liquid from cucumber slices a few at a time, and place slices in the bowl. Discard liquid. Add lemon juice mixture, green onions, and yogurt. Mix and sprinkle additional paprika or dill over top. Chill for 1-2 hours.

Chicken, Roasted Veggies & Arugula Salad

Serves 2

Ingredients - Allergies: SF, GF, DF, EF, NF

- 1 cup sliced grilled chicken
- 1/2 cup tomato
- 1/2 cup grilled veggies
- 1 cup arugula
- 1/2 cup chopped red peppers

Dressing:

- 1 tbsp. olive oil or avocado oil
- 1 tbsp. fresh lemon juice
- pinch of black pepper
- pinch of sea salt

Instructions: Mix all ingredients.

Tuna, Tomato, Arugula & Eggs Salad

Serves 2

Ingredients - Allergies: SF, GF, DF, NF

- 1 cup tuna chunks
- 1/2 cup chopped tomato
- 2 halved eggs
- 1 cup Arugula
- 1/2 cup sliced yellow peppers

Dressing:

- 1 tbsp. olive oil
- 1 tbsp. fresh lemon juice
- pinch of black pepper
- pinch of sea salt

Instructions: Mix all ingredients.

DANCES
WALKER

Chicken, Tomato, Spinach & Cucumber Salad

Serves 2

Ingredients - Allergies: SF, GF, DF, EF, NF, V

- 1 cup grilled chicken
- 1/2 cup chopped cucumber
- 1/2 cup chopped tomato
- 1 cup cooked spinach

Dressing:
- 1 tbsp. olive oil or avocado oil
- 1 tbsp. fresh lemon juice
- pinch of black pepper
- pinch of sea salt

Instructions: Mix all ingredients.

Artichoke, Arugula & Lamb Salad

Serves 2

Ingredients - Allergies: SF, GF, DF, EF, NF

- 1 cup sliced roasted lamb
- 1 cup roasted quartered artichoke hearts.
- 1/2 cup chopped red onion
- 1 cup Arugula

Dressing:

- 1 tbsp. olive oil or avocado oil
- 1 tbsp. fresh lemon juice
- pinch of black pepper
- pinch of sea salt

Instructions: Roast artichoke hearts for 20 minutes in the oven. Mix all ingredients.

Tuna, Tomato, Eggs & Lettuce Salad

Serves 2

Ingredients - Allergies: SF, GF, DF, NF

- 1 cup tuna
- 2 boiled eggs, sliced
- 1 cup chopped tomato
- 1 cup lettuce

***Dressing*:**

- 1 tbsp. olive oil or avocado oil
- 1 tbsp. fresh lemon juice
- pinch of black pepper
- pinch of sea salt

Instructions: Mix all ingredients.

Greek Salad

Serves 4 - Allergies: SF, GF, EF, NF

- 1 head iceberg lettuce
- 1 head romaine lettuce
- 1 lb. plump tomatoes
- 6 oz. Greek or black olives, sliced
- 4 oz. sliced radishes
- 4 oz. low-fat feta or goat cheese
- 2 oz. anchovies (optional)

Dressing:

- 3 oz. olive oil or avocado oil
- 3 oz. fresh lemon juice
- 1 tsp. dried oregano
- 1 tsp. black pepper
- 1 tsp. salt
- 4 cloves garlic, minced

Wash and cut lettuce into pieces. Slice tomatoes in quarters. Combine olives, lettuce, tomatoes, and radishes in large bowl. Mix dressing ingredients together and toss with vegetables. Pour out into a shallow serving bowl. Crumble feta/goat cheese over all, and arrange anchovy fillets on top (if desired).

Superfoods Stews, Chilies and Curries

Barbecued Beef

Serves 8

Ingredients - Allergies: SF, GF, DF, EF, NF

- 1-1/2 cups tomato paste
- 1/4 cup lemon juice
- 2 tbsp. mustard
- 1/2 tsp. salt
- 1/4 tsp. ground black pepper
- 1/2 tsp. minced garlic
- 4 pounds boneless chuck roast

Instructions

Place chuck roast in a slow cooker. Pour all ingredients over and mix well. Cover, and cook on low for 7 to 9 hours.

Superfoods Chili

Serves 6

Ingredients - Allergies: SF, GF, DF, EF, NF

- 2 tbsp. coconut oil
- 2 onions, chopped
- 3 cloves garlic, minced
- 1 pound ground beef
- 3/4 pound beef sirloin, cubed
- 1 cup diced tomatoes
- 1 cup strong brewed coffee
- ½ cup tomato paste
- 2 cups beef broth
- 1 tbsp. cumin seeds
- 1 tbsp. unsweetened cocoa powder
- 1 tsp. dried oregano
- 1 tsp. ground cayenne pepper
- 1 tsp. ground coriander
- 1 tsp. salt
- 3 cups cooked kidney beans
- 4 fresh hot chili peppers, chopped

Instructions

Put all ingredients in the slow cooker and cook on low for 4 hours.

Superfoods Goulash

Serves 4-6

Ingredients - Allergies: SF, GF, DF, EF, NF

- 3 cups cauliflower
- 1 pound ground beef
- 1 medium onion, chopped
- salt to taste
- ground black pepper to taste
- garlic to taste
- 2 cups cooked cannellini beans
- 1/2 cup tomato paste

Put all ingredients in the slow cooker and cook on low for 4 hours.

Chicken Cacciatore

Serves 8

Ingredients - Allergies: SF, GF, DF, EF, NF

- 4 pounds of chicken thighs, with skin on
- 2 Tbsp. extra virgin olive oil or avocado oil
- Salt
- 1 sliced onion
- 1/3 cup white wine (optional)
- 1 sliced red or green bell pepper
- 8 ounces sliced cremini mushrooms
- 2 sliced garlic cloves
- 1 cup peeled and chopped tomatoes
- 1/2 tsp. ground black pepper
- 1 tsp. dry oregano
- 1 tsp. dry thyme
- 1 sprig fresh rosemary
- 1 tbsp. fresh parsley

Instructions

Put all ingredients in the slow cooker and cook on low for 4 hours.

Cabbage Stewed with Meat

Serves 8

Ingredients - Allergies: SF, GF, DF, EF, NF

- 1-1/2 pounds ground beef
- 1 cup beef stock
- 1 chopped onion
- 1 bay leaf
- 1/4 tsp. pepper
- 2 sliced celery ribs
- 4 cups shredded cabbage
- 1 carrot, sliced
- 1/2 cup tomato paste
- 1/4 tsp. salt

Instructions

Put all ingredients in the slow cooker and cook on low for 4 hours.

Beef Stew with Peas and Carrots

Serves 8

Ingredients - Allergies: SF, GF, DF, EF, NF

- 1 cup chopped carrots
- 1 cup chopped onions
- 2 tbsp. coconut oil
- 1-1/2 cups green peas
- 4 cups beef stock
- 1/2 tsp. salt
- 1/4 tsp. ground black pepper
- 1/2 tsp. minced garlic
- 4 pounds boneless chuck roast

Instructions

Put all ingredients in the slow cooker and cook on low for 6 hours.

Green Chicken Stew

Serves 6-8

Ingredients - Allergies: SF, GF, DF, EF, NF

- 1-1/2 cups broccoli florets
- 1 cup chopped celery stalks
- 1 cup sliced leeks
- 2 tbsp. coconut oil
- 1-1/2 cups green peas
- 2 cups chicken stock
- 1/2 tsp. salt
- 1/4 tsp. ground black pepper
- 1/2 tsp. minced garlic
- 4 pounds boneless skinless chicken pieces

Instructions

Put all ingredients in the slow cooker and cook on low for 4 hours.

Irish Stew

Serves 8

Ingredients - Allergies: SF, GF, DF, EF, NF

- 2 chopped onions
- 2 Tbsp. coconut oil
- 1 sprig dried thyme
- 2 1/2 pounds chopped meat from lamb neck
- 3 chopped carrots
- 4 cups chicken stock
- Salt
- Ground black pepper
- 1 bouquet garni (thyme, parsley and bay leaf)
- 1 bunch chopped parsley
- 1 bunch chives

Instructions

Put all ingredients in the slow cooker and cook on low for 6 hours.

Hungarian Pea Stew

Serves 8

Ingredients - Allergies: SF, GF, DF, EF, NF

- 5 cups green peas
- 1 pound cubed pork
- 2 tbsp olive oil or avocado oil
- 2 1/2 tbsp almond flour (optional)
- 2 tbsp chopped parsley
- 1 cup water
- 1/2 tsp salt
- 1 cup coconut milk

Instructions

Put all ingredients in the slow cooker and cook on low for 6 hours.

Greek Beef Stew (Stifado)

Serves 8

Ingredients - Allergies: SF, GF, DF, EF, NF

- 4 large pieces of veal or beef osso bucco
- 20 whole shallots, peeled
- 3 bay leaves
- 8 garlic cloves
- 3 sprigs rosemary
- 6 whole pimentos
- 5 whole cloves
- 1/2 tsp ground nutmeg
- 1/2 cup olive oil or avocado oil
- 1/3 cup apple cider vinegar
- 1 tbsp. salt
- 1 cup tomato paste
- 1/4 tsp black pepper

Instructions

Put all ingredients in the slow cooker and cook on low for 8 hours.

Beef, Parsnip, Celery Stew

Serves 8

Ingredients - Allergies: SF, GF, DF, EF, NF

- 2 1/2 pounds cubed beef meat
- 2 chopped onions
- 2 chopped carrots
- 2 Tbsp. coconut oil
- 1 sprig dried thyme
- 2 chopped parsnips
- 4 cups beef stock
- Salt
- Ground black pepper
- 1 bouquet garni (thyme, parsley and bay leaf)
- 1 bunch chopped parsley
- 1 bunch chives

Instructions

Put all ingredients in the slow cooker and cook on low for 8 hours.

Vegetarian Chili

Serves 4-6

Ingredients - Allergies: SF, GF, DF, EF, V, NF

1 tbsp. coconut oil
1/2 cup chopped onions
3/4 cup chopped carrots
3 cloves garlic, minced
1 cup chopped green bell pepper
1 cup chopped red bell pepper
3/4 cup chopped celery
1 tbsp. chili powder
2 cups cauliflower florets
1 cup chopped tomatoes
2 cups raw black beans
1 tbsp. ground cumin
1-1/2 teaspoons oregano
1-1/2 teaspoons crushed basil leaves

Instructions

Put all ingredients in the slow cooker and cook on low for 8 hours.

Lentil Stew

Serves 6-8

Ingredients - Allergies: SF, GF, DF, EF, NF

- 2 cup dry lentils
- 6 cups chicken broth
- 1 tomato
- 1 medium parsnip chopped + 1/2 cup chopped carrot
- 1/2 cup chopped onion + 1/2 cup chopped celery (optional)
- a few sprigs of parsley and basil + 1 garlic clove (minced)
- 2 pound of cubed lean pork or beef + pepper to taste

Instructions: Dump everything in a slow cooker and cook on low for 3 hours.

Braised Green Peas with Beef

Serves 4

Ingredients - Allergies: SF, GF, DF, EF, NF

- 2 cups fresh or frozen green peas
- 2 onions, finely chopped
- 2 cloves of garlic, chopped and 1/2 inch of peeled and chopped fresh ginger (optional)
- 1/2 tsp. red pepper flakes, or to taste
- 1 tomato, roughly chopped
- 1 chopped carrot
- 2 tbsp. coconut oil
- 1 cup chicken broth
- 1 pound cubed beef
- Salt and freshly ground black pepper (to taste)

Put all ingredients in the slow cooker and cook on low for 4 hours.

White Chicken Chili

Serves: 5

Ingredients - Allergies: SF, GF, DF, EF, NF

- 4 large boneless, skinless chicken breasts
- 2 green bell peppers
- 1 large yellow onion
- 1 jalapeno
- 1/2 cup diced green chilies (optional)
- 1/2 cup of spring onions
- 1.5 tbsp. coconut oil
- 3 cups cooked cannellini beans
- 3.5 cups chicken or vegetable broth
- 1 tsp. ground cumin
- 1/4 tsp. cayenne pepper
- salt to taste

Instructions

Put all ingredients in the slow cooker and cook on low for 4 hours.

Kale Pork

Serves 4

Ingredients - Allergies: SF, GF, DF, EF, NF

- 1 tbsp. coconut oil
- 1 pound pork tenderloin, trimmed and cut into 1-inch pieces
- 3/4 tsp. salt
- 1 medium onion, finely chopped
- 4 cloves garlic, minced
- 2 teaspoons paprika
- 1/4 tsp. crushed red pepper (optional)
- 1 cup white wine
- 1 plum tomato, chopped
- 4 cups chicken broth
- 1 bunch kale, chopped
- 2 cups cooked cannellini beans

Instructions

Put all ingredients in the slow cooker and cook on low for 4 hours.

Braised Green Beans with Pork

Serves 2

Ingredients - Allergies: SF, GF, DF, EF, NF

- 2 cups fresh or frozen green beans
- 1 onion, finely chopped
- 2 cloves of garlic, thinly sliced
- 1/2 inch of peeled/sliced fresh ginger
- 1/2 tsp. red pepper flakes, or to taste
- 1 tomato, roughly chopped
- 1 tbsp. coconut oil
- 1/2 cup chicken broth
- Salt and ground black pepper
- 1/4 lemon, cut into wedges, to serve
- 1 pound lean pork

Instructions

Cut each bean in half. Put all ingredients in the slow cooker and cook on low for 4 hours.

Chicken Mushrooms & Olives Stew

Serves 6

Ingredients - Allergies: SF, GF, DF, EF, NF

- 4 pounds chicken with skin on
- 1/2 cups chopped carrots
- 1 cup chopped onions
- 2 tbsp. coconut oil
- 1 cup sliced mushrooms
- 1/2 cup chopped celery
- 1 cup black olives
- 1/2 tsp. salt
- 1/4 tsp. ground black pepper
- 1/2 tsp. minced garlic
- ½ cup fresh parsley

Instructions

Put all ingredients in the crockpot, cover and cook on low 6 hours.

Chicken Pasanda Curry

Serves: 6

Ingredients - Allergies: SF, GF, DF, EF, NF

- 2 cups cubed chicken meat
- Curry Paste, but go low on the heat
- 2 cups tomato paste
- 1/2 cup coconut milk or cream
- Cilantro for garnishing

Instructions

Make Curry Paste. Add the tomato paste, chicken and the cream. Stir to combine, add to crockpot and cook on low for 3 hours.

Osso Bucco & Garlic Stew

Serves 6-8

Ingredients - Allergies: SF, GF, DF, EF, NF

- 10 cloves garlic
- 2 cups chopped onions
- 1 chopped carrot
- 1 cup chopped celery
- 2 tbsp. coconut oil
- 2 cups beef stock
- 1/2 tsp. salt
- 1/4 tsp. ground black pepper
- 1 tsp. chopped parsley
- 4 pounds osso bucco

Instructions

Put all ingredients in the slow cooker and cook on low for 8 hours.

Duck Stew

Serves 8

Ingredients - Allergies: SF, GF, DF, EF, NF

- 2 Tbsp. olive oil
- 2 pound chopped duck meat (1/2 inch wide)
- 1/2 pound duck liver, sliced
- 1 chopped carrot
- 1 cup chopped celery
- 1 cup chopped onions
- 3 garlic cloves, chopped
- 2 cups chicken broth
- 1 cup sliced shiitake mushrooms
- 1/2 cup cilantro

Instructions

Put all ingredients in the slow cooker and cook on low for 4 Hrs.

Slow cooked Squash, Cauliflower and Peppers Coconut Curry

Serves: 6

Ingredients - Allergies: SF, GF, NF

- Curry Paste – see recipe
- 3 cups peeled, chopped squash
- 2 cups thick coconut milk
- 3 tbsp. coconut oil
- 2 tbsp. lucuma powder
- 2 pounds tomatoes
- 1 cup chopped Cauliflower
- 1 cup chopped Green Peppers
- Cilantro for topping

Instructions

Put all ingredients in the slow cooker and cook on low for 4 Hrs.

Ratatouille

Serves 4-6

Ingredients - Allergies: SF, GF, NF

- 2 large eggplants, sliced
- 2 medium onions, sliced
- 2 red or green peppers, sliced
- 4 large tomatoes, sliced
- 2 cloves garlic, crushed
- 4 tbsp. coconut oil
- 1 tbsp. fresh basil
- Salt and freshly milled black pepper

Instructions

Put all ingredients in the slow cooker and cook on low for 4 Hrs.

Pork, Celery and Basil Stew

Serves 8

Ingredients - Allergies: SF, GF, DF, EF, NF

- 1 cup chopped onions
- 2 Tbsp. coconut oil
- 2 1/2 pounds chopped pork meat
- 1 chopped carrot
- 2 cups beef stock
- 1 cup white wine (optional)
- Salt
- Ground black pepper
- 1 bunch chopped parsley
- 1 cup chopped celery
- 1/2 cup fresh basil

Instructions

Add all ingredients to slow cooker and cook on low for 8 hours.

Slow cooked Chia, Flax & Broccoli

Serves 4

Ingredients - Allergies: SF, GF, DF, EF, NF

- 2 cups broccoli florets
- 1 cup chopped onions
- 2 tbsp. coconut oil
- 1 cup Healthy Superfoods Casserole Sauce
- 1/2 cup flax seeds meal
- 1/4 cup chia seeds

Instructions

Put broccoli and onions in the slow cooker dish, mix sauce cream, flax and chia seeds, pour sauce on top, cover and cook on low for 3 hours.

Slow cooked Chicken & Tomato Casserole

Serves 4

Ingredients - Allergies: SF, GF, DF, EF, NF

- 1-1/2 cups chopped chicken meat
- 1/2 cup chopped onions
- 2 tbsp. coconut oil
- 1 cup sliced tomatoes
- 1 cup Healthy Superfoods Casserole Sauce
- 1 Tbsp. chopped parsley

Instructions

Put all recipe ingredients (except sauce) in the slow cooker dish, pour sauce on top, arrange sliced tomatoes on top, cover and cook on low for 4 hours. Garnish with parsley.

Slow cooked Eggplant, Zucchini and Tomato

Serves 4

Ingredients - Allergies: SF, GF, DF, EF, NF

- 1-1/2 cups sliced zucchini
- 1-1/2 cups sliced tomatoes
- 2 tbsp. coconut oil
- 1-1/2 cups sliced eggplant
- 1/2 tsp. salt
- 1/4 tsp. ground black pepper
- 1/2 tsp. minced garlic

Instructions

Arrange all ingredients in the slow cooker dish, cover and cook on low for 4 hours.

Slow cooked Zucchini

Serves 4

Ingredients - Allergies: SF, GF, DF, EF, NF

- 1-1/2 cups sliced zucchini
- 1 cup chopped onions
- 2 tbsp. coconut oil
- 2 tbsp. chopped green onions
- 1 cup Healthy Superfoods Casserole Sauce

Instructions

Put ingredients in the casserole dish, pour sauce on top, cover and bake for 1 1/2 hours on 400F. Sprinkle with green onions before serving.

Slow cooked Red Peppers, Zucchini and Eggplant

Serves 4

Ingredients - Allergies: SF, GF, DF, EF, NF

- 1 chopped carrots
- 1 - 1/2 cup chopped onions
- 1 - 1/2 cup sliced red peppers
- 4 tbsp. coconut oil
- 1 cup sliced zucchini
- 1/2 tsp. salt
- 1/4 tsp. ground black pepper
- 1/2 tsp. minced garlic
- 1/2 tsp. oregano
- 2 pounds sliced eggplant
- 1/2 cup Tomato Paste

Instructions

Put all ingredients in the slow cooker and cook on low for 4 Hrs.

Meat Stew with Red Beans

Serves 8

Ingredients - Allergies: SF, GF, DF, EF, NF

- 3 tbsp. olive oil or avocado oil
- 1/2 cup chopped onion
- 1 lb lean cubed stewing beef
- 2 tsp. ground cumin
- 2 tsp. ground turmeric (optional)
- 1/2 tsp. ground cinnamon (optional)
- 2 1/2 cups water
- 5 tbsp. chopped fresh parsley
- 3 tbsp. snipped chives
- 2 cups cooked kidney beans
- 1 lemon, juice of
- 1 tbsp. almond flour
- salt and black pepper

Instructions

Put all ingredients in the slow cooker and cook on low for 4 Hrs.

Slow Cooker Pepper Steak

Serves 4-6

Ingredients - Allergies: SF, GF, DF, EF, NF

- 2 pounds beef sirloin, cut into 2 inch strips
- 1 tbsp. minced garlic
- 3 tbsp. coconut oil
- 1 cup Beef Broth
- 1 tbsp. tapioca flour (optional)
- 1/2 cup chopped onion
- 1 cup carrots
- 1 cup chopped tomatoes
- 1 tsp. salt

Instructions

Sprinkle beef with minced garlic. Heat the coconut oil in a skillet and brown the seasoned beef sirloin strips. Transfer to a slow cooker.

Add carrots, onion, chopped tomatoes and salt. Mix in tapioca flour in broth until dissolved. Pour broth into the slow cooker with meat. Cover and cook on high for 3 to 4 hours, or on low for 6 to 8 hours.

Pork Tenderloin with peppers and onions

Serves 3-4

Ingredients - Allergies: SF, GF, DF, EF, NF

- 1 tbsp. coconut oil
- 1 pound pork loin
- 1 tbsp. caraway seeds
- 1/2 tsp sea salt
- 1/4 tsp ground black pepper
- 1 red onion, thinly sliced
- 2 red bell peppers, sliced
- 2 cloves of garlic, minced
- 1/4-1/3 cup chicken broth

Instructions

Wash and chop vegetables. Slice pork loin, and season with black pepper, caraway seeds and sea salt. Heat a pan over medium heat. Add coconut oil when hot. Add pork loin and brown slightly. Add onions and mushrooms, and continue to sauté until onions are translucent. Add peppers, garlic and chicken broth. Simmer until vegetables are tender and pork is fully cooked.

Beef Bourguinon

Serves 8-10

Ingredients - Allergies: SF, GF, DF, EF

- 4 pounds cubed lean beef
- 1 cup red wine (optional)
- 1/3 cup coconut oil
- 1 tsp. thyme
- 1 tsp. black pepper
- 2 cloves garlic, crushed
- 1 onion, diced
- 1 pound mushrooms, sliced
- 1 Tbsp. almond flour (optional)

Instructions

Marinate beef in wine, oil, thyme and pepper for few hours at room temperature or 6-8 hours in the fridge. Add beef with marinade and all other ingredients to a crock pot. Cook on low for 7-9 hrs.

Italian Chicken

Serves 6-8

Ingredients - Allergies: SF, GF, DF, EF

- 1 skinless chicken, cut into pieces
- 1 Tbsp. almond flour (optional)
- 1 1/2 tsp. salt
- 1/8 tsp. pepper
- 1/2 cup chicken broth
- 1 cup sliced mushrooms
- 1/2 tsp. paprika
- 1 zucchini, sliced into medium pieces
- ground black pepper
- parsley to garnish

Instructions

Season chicken with 1 tsp. salt. Combine flour, pepper, remaining salt, and paprika. Coat chicken pieces with this mixture. Place zucchini first in a crockpot. Pour broth over zucchini. Arrange chicken on top. Cover and cook on low for 6 to 8 hours or until tender. Turn control to high, add mushrooms, cover, and cook on high for additional 10-15 minutes. Garnish with parsley and ground black pepper.

Ropa Vieja

Ingredients - Allergies: SF, GF, DF, EF, NF

6 servings

- 1 tbsp. coconut oil
- 2 pounds beef flank steak
- 1 cup beef broth
- 1 cup tomato sauce
- 1 small onion, sliced
- 1 green bell pepper sliced into strips
- 2 cloves garlic, chopped
- 1/2 cup tomato paste
- 1 tsp. ground cumin
- 1 tsp. chopped cilantro
- 1 tbsp. olive oil & 1 tbsp. lemon juice

Instructions

Add all ingredients to a crock pot. Cover, and cook on high for 4 hours, or on Low for up to 8 hours.

Lemon Roast Chicken

Serves 6-8

Ingredients - Allergies: SF, GF, DF, EF, NF

- 1 whole skinless chicken
- 1 dash Salt
- 1 dash Pepper
- 1 tsp. Oregano
- 2 cloves minced garlic
- 2 tbsp. coconut oil
- 1/4 cup Water
- 3 tbsp. Lemon juice
- Rosemary

Instructions

Add ingredients to a crock pot and cover. Cook on low 7 hours. Add lemon juice when cooking is done.

Fall Lamb and Vegetable Stew

Serves 6-8

Ingredients - Allergies: SF, GF, DF, EF, NF

- 2 pounds Lamb stew meat
- 1 chopped Tomato
- 1 cup green beans
- 1 cup carrots, sliced
- 1/2 cup green peas
- 1 cup Onions, chopped
- 2 teaspoons Salt
- 1 each Garlic cloves, crushed
- 1/2 tsp. Thyme leaves
- 1 each Bay leaves
- 2 cups chicken broth

Instructions

Cut green beans. Place vegetables and lamb in crockpot. Mix salt, garlic, thyme, and bay leaf into broth and pour over lamb and vegetables. Cover and cook on low for 7 hours.

Slow cooker pork loin

Serves 4-6

Ingredients - Allergies: SF, GF, DF, EF, NF

- 1-1/2 lb pork loin
- 1 cup tomato sauce
- 2 zucchinis, sliced
- 1 head cauliflower, separated into medium florets
- 1-2 Tbs dried basil
- 1/4 tsp ground black pepper
- 1/2 tsp sea salt (optional)

Instructions

Add all of the ingredients to a crock pot.

Cook on high for 3-4 hours or low 7-8 hours.

Pork, Zucchini, Pork, Tomato & Corn Stew

Serves 8

Ingredients - Allergies: SF, GF, DF, EF, NF

- 1/2 cups cooked corn (optional)
- 1 cup chopped onions
- 1-1/2 cups sliced zucchini
- 1 cup chopped tomato
- 2 tbsp. coconut oil
- 2 tbsp. chopped garlic
- 2 tsp. salt and 1 tsp. ground pepper
- 4 pounds cubed pork

Instructions

Put ingredients in the slow cooker. Cover, and cook on low for 7 to 9 hours.

Red Peppers Pork Curry

Serves 8

Ingredients - Allergies: SF, GF, DF, EF, NF

- 3 cups sliced red peppers
- 1 cup chopped onions
- 2 tbsp. coconut oil
- 1 cup curry paste*
- 4 pounds chopped pork meat

Instructions

Put ingredients in the slow cooker. Cover, and cook on low for 7 to 9 hours.

Beef Ratatouille

Serves 8

Ingredients - Allergies: SF, GF, DF, EF, NF

- 1-1/2 cups sliced zucchini
- 1 cup chopped onions
- 1-1/2 cups sliced eggplant
- 1-1/2 cups sliced red peppers (or tomato)
- 2 tbsp. coconut oil
- 2 tbsp. chopped garlic
- 2 tsp. salt and 1 tsp. ground pepper
- 4 pounds cubed beef

Instructions

Put ingredients in the slow cooker. Cover, and cook on low for 7 to 9 hours.

Chicken, Green Peas and Red Peppers Stew

Serves 8

Ingredients - Allergies: SF, GF, DF, EF, NF

- 1 cup green peas
- 1 cup chopped onions
- 1-1/2 cups sliced red peppers
- 2 tbsp. coconut oil
- 2 cups chicken broth
- 2 tsp. salt and 1 tsp. ground pepper
- 4 pounds cubed chicken

Instructions

Put ingredients in the slow cooker. Cover, and cook on low for 7 to 9 hours.

Crock Pot Turkey Roast Mediterranean style

Serves 8

Ingredients - Allergies: SF, GF, DF, EF, NF

- 1/2 cup Kalamata olives
- 1/2 cup chopped sun dried tomatoes
- 1 cup chicken broth
- 2 garlic cloves, minced
- 1 cup chopped onions
- 2 tbsp. coconut oil
- 4 pounds turkey breast
- Rub thyme, salt and ground black pepper.

Instructions

Put ingredients in the slow cooker. Cover, and cook on low for 7 to 9 hours.

Slow Cooker Pot Roast

Serves 8

Ingredients - Allergies: SF, GF, DF, EF, NF

- 1 cup sliced celery
- 1 cup chopped carrot
- 3 cups beef broth
- 1 cup red wine (optional) & 3 garlic cloves (optional)
- 1 cup chopped onions
- 2 tbsp. coconut oil
- 4 pounds beef chuck roast
- Rub thyme, salt and ground black pepper. Add 1 bay leaf.

Instructions

Put ingredients in the slow cooker. Cover, and cook on low for 7 to 9 hours.

Crock Pot Whole Chicken

Serves 8

Ingredients - Allergies: SF, GF, DF, EF, NF

- 1 cup sliced celery
- 1 cup chopped carrot
- 1 cup chopped parsnip (optional)
- 2 cups chopped onions
- 2 tbsp. coconut oil
- 1 whole chicken with skin on
- Rub paprika, salt and ground black pepper on the chicken skin and inside. Optionally add lemon quarters inside.

Instructions

Put veggies in the slow cooker and place chicken on top. Cover, and cook on low for 7 to 9 hours.

Chicken in Sun Dried Tomato Sauce

Serves 8

Ingredients - Allergies: SF, GF, DF, EF, NF

- 12 sun dried tomatoes, chopped
- 1 cup coconut cream or full fat coconut milk
- 1 cup chicken broth
- 1/2 cup white wine (optional)
- a pinch of dried thyme and oregano
- 2 tbsp. coconut oil
- Salt and ground black pepper to taste
- 4 pounds dark chicken meat

Instructions

Put ingredients in the slow cooker. Cover, and cook on low for 7 to 9 hours.

Corn, Mushrooms Chicken Stew

Serves 8

Ingredients - Allergies: SF, GF, DF, EF, NF

- 2 cups sliced mushrooms
- 1 cups chopped onions
- 1 cup corn (optional)
- 2 tbsp. coconut oil
- 2 cups tomato paste*
- Salt and ground black pepper to taste
- 4 pounds chicken meat

Instructions

Put ingredients in the slow cooker. Cover, and cook on low for 7 to 9 hours.

Chicken and Baby Carrots Stew

Serves 8

Ingredients - Allergies: SF, GF, DF, EF, NF

- 1 & 1/2 cups baby carrots
- 1 cup chopped onions
- 2 tbsp. coconut oil
- Salt, ground black pepper to taste
- 4 pounds dark chicken meat

Instructions

Put ingredients in the slow cooker. Cover, and cook on low for 7 to 9 hours.

Pork White Bean Chili

Serves 8

Ingredients - Allergies: SF, GF, DF, EF, NF

- 2 cups sliced red peppers
- 1 cup chopped onions
- 2 tbsp. coconut oil
- 1 cup uncooked cannellini beans
- 1/4 cup sliced jalapeno peppers (adjust heat to taste)
- 1 cup sweet corn (optional)
- Salt, ground black pepper and ground cumin to taste
- 2-3 cups beef stock
- 4 pounds minced pork meat

Instructions

Put ingredients in the slow cooker. Cover, and cook on low for 7 to 9 hours.

Pork Meat Stew

Serves 8

Ingredients - Allergies: SF, GF, DF, EF, NF

- 2 tomatoes, sliced
- 1 cup chopped onions
- 2 tbsp. coconut oil
- 2 large red peppers, sliced
- 1 bunch chopped parsley
- Salt, ground black pepper and ground cumin to taste
- 1 cup beef stock
- 4 pounds cubed pork meat

Instructions

Put ingredients in the slow cooker. Cover, and cook on low for 7 to 9 hours.

Lamb & Zucchini Stew

Serves 8

Ingredients - Allergies: SF, GF, DF, EF, NF

- 2 medium zucchinis, sliced
- 1 cup chopped onions
- 2 tbsp. coconut oil
- 2 sliced tomatoes & 2 yellow peppers, sliced
- 2 Tbsp. chopped rosemary
- Salt, ground black pepper and ground cumin to taste
- 1 cup beef stock
- 4 pounds cubed lamb meat

Instructions

Put ingredients in the slow cooker. Cover, and cook on low for 7 to 9 hours.

Seafood Stew

Serves 8

Ingredients - Allergies: SF, GF, DF, EF, NF

- 3/4 cup coconut oil
- 2 onions, chopped
- 1 pound peeled and deveined large shrimp
- 1 pound bay scallops
- 15 cleaned and debearded mussels
- 1 cup crabmeat
- 2 cloves garlic, minced
- 1,5 cups stewed tomatoes
- 1 cup fish broth
- 2 bay leaves
- 1/2 tsp. dried oregano
- 1 cup water
- 1 lemon cut in wedges
- 1-1/2 cups white wine

Instructions

Put ingredients in the slow cooker. Cover, and cook on low for 7 to 9 hours.

Chicken, Mushrooms & Carrots Stew

Serves 8

Ingredients - Allergies: SF, GF, DF, EF, NF

- 2 cups halved mushrooms
- 1 cup chopped onions
- 2 tbsp. coconut oil
- 1 cup chopped carrots
- Salt, ground black pepper to taste
- 1 cup chicken stock
- 4 pounds cubed chicken meat

Instructions

Put ingredients in the slow cooker. Cover, and cook on low for 7 to 9 hours.

Cabbage & Mushrooms Beef Stew

Serves 8

Ingredients - Allergies: SF, GF, DF, EF, NF

- 2 cups sliced mushrooms
- 1 cup chopped onions & 1 cup chopped carrot
- 2 tbsp. coconut oil
- 2 cups sauerkraut
- Salt, ground black pepper and ground cumin to taste
- 2 cups beef stock
- 2 pounds ground beef

Instructions

Put ingredients in the slow cooker and mix. Cover, and cook on low for 7 to 9 hours.

Shiitake & Chicken Stew

Serves 8

Ingredients - Allergies: SF, GF, DF, EF, NF

- 2 cups whole shiitake mushrooms
- 1 cup chopped leeks
- 2 tbsp. coconut oil
- Salt, ground black pepper to taste
- 3 cups chicken stock
- 4 pounds cubed chicken meat

Instructions

Put ingredients in the slow cooker. Cover, and cook on low for 7 to 9 hours.

Creamy Mushroom Chicken Stew

Serves 8

Ingredients - Allergies: SF, GF, DF, EF, NF

- 1 cup full fat coconut milk
- 1 cup chopped onions & 2 garlic cloves, minced
- 4 tbsp. coconut oil
- 1/2 cup chopped carrot
- Salt, ground black pepper and fresh thyme to taste
- 2 cups mixed Portobello and white button mushrooms
- 1 cup beef stock
- 4 pounds chopped chicken meat

Instructions

Put ingredients in the slow cooker. Cover, and cook on low for 7 to 9 hours.

Chicken & Green Beans Stew

Serves 8

Ingredients - Allergies: SF, GF, DF, EF, NF

- 2 cups green beans cut into 2 inch pieces
- 1 cup chopped onions
- 2 tbsp. coconut oil
- Salt, ground black pepper to taste
- 1 cup chicken stock
- 1 cup chopped tomato
- 1 Tbsp. parsley
- 4 pounds chicken breast meat cut into stripes

Instructions

Put ingredients in the slow cooker. Cover, and cook on low for 7 to 9 hours.

Beef Liver Stew

Serves 8

Ingredients - Allergies: SF, GF, DF, EF, NF

- 2 cups chopped onions
- 2 tbsp. coconut oil
- 3 garlic cloves, minced
- 1 grated carrot
- Salt, ground black pepper and ground cumin taste
- 2 cups chicken stock
- 1 cup red wine (optional)
- 1 tsp. turmeric (optional)
- 4 pounds Beef liver cut in stripes

Instructions

Put ingredients in the slow cooker. Cover, and cook on low for 7 to 9 hours.

Venison & Green Peas Stew

Serves 8

Ingredients - Allergies: SF, GF, DF, EF, NF

- 2 cups green peas
- 2 cups chopped onions
- 2 tbsp. coconut oil
- 1 cup chopped carrot
- Salt, ground black pepper and ground cumin to taste
- 2 cups beef stock
- 4 pounds venison meat

Instructions

Put ingredients in the slow cooker. Cover, and cook on low for 7 to 9 hours.

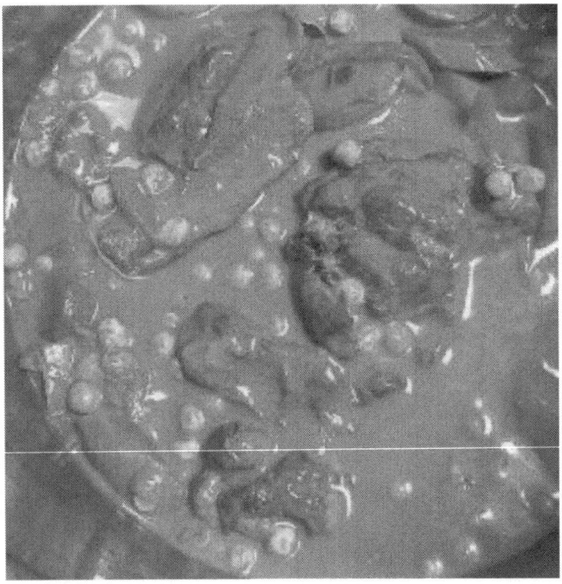

Pork Broccoli

Serves 8

Ingredients - Allergies: SF, GF, DF, EF, NF

- 2 cups chopped onions
- 2 tbsp. coconut oil
- 3 cups broccoli
- Salt, ground black pepper and 1 Tbsp. chopped garlic
- 2 cups beef stock
- 4 pounds Pork roast

Instructions

Put ingredients in the slow cooker. Cover, and cook on low for 7 to 9 hours.

Pork & Leeks

Serves 8

Ingredients - Allergies: SF, GF, DF, EF, NF

- 2 cups chopped carrot
- 2 tbsp. coconut oil
- 3 cups chopped leeks
- Salt, ground black pepper and ground cumin to taste
- 2 cups beef stock
- 4 pounds cubed pork meat

Instructions

Put ingredients in the slow cooker. Cover, and cook on low for 7 to 9 hours.

Italian Beef

Serves 8

Ingredients - Allergies: SF, GF, DF, EF, NF

- 2 cups red peppers, sliced
- 2 cups chopped onions
- 2 tbsp. coconut oil
- Salt, ground black pepper and ground cumin to taste
- 2 bay leaves, 2 Tbsp. chopped garlic, 1 tsp. oregano, dried basil and dried parsley each (optional)
- 2 cups beef stock
- 4 pounds beef chuck (rump) roast

Instructions

Put ingredients in the slow cooker. Cover, and cook on low for 9 hours.

Jerk Chicken

Serves 8

Ingredients - Allergies: SF, GF, DF, EF, NF

- 2 cup sliced green peppers
- 2 cups chopped onions
- 2 tbsp. coconut oil
- Salt, ground black pepper and ground allspice to taste
- 2 cups chicken stock
- 4 pounds cubed chicken meat
- 1 lime - juice & 1 or more Scotch bonnet peppers (to taste).
- 2 Tbsp. minced ginger & 2 Tbsp. minced garlic.
- 1 Tsp. cinnamon & a pinch of nutmeg.

Instructions

Put ingredients in the slow cooker. Cover, and cook on low for 8 hours.

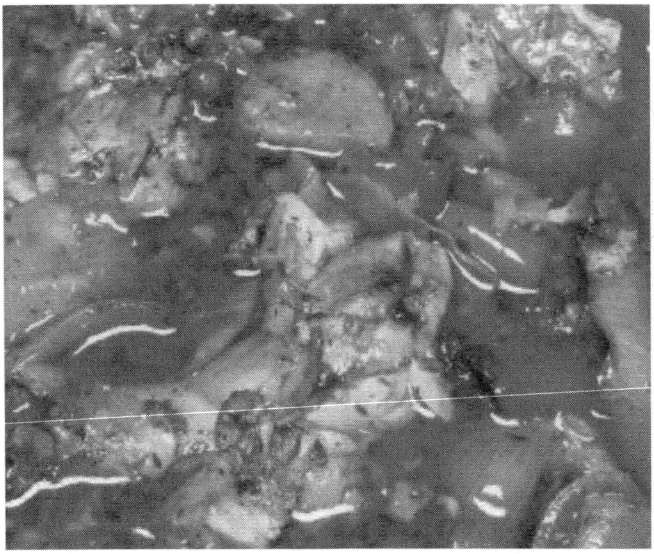

Cauliflower Beef & Carrot

Serves 8

Ingredients - Allergies: SF, GF, DF, EF, NF

- 2 cup chopped carrots
- 2 cups chopped red onions
- 2 tbsp. coconut oil
- 2 cups cauliflower florets
- Salt, ground black pepper and ground cumin to taste
- 2 cups beef stock
- 4 pounds cubed beef meat

Instructions

Put ingredients in the slow cooker. Cover, and cook on low for 7 to 9 hours.

Eggplant, Tripe & Broccoli

Serves 8

Ingredients - Allergies: SF, GF, DF, EF, NF

- 2 cups eggplant, sliced
- 1 cup chopped onions
- 1 cup broccoli
- 1 cup green beans
- 2 tbsp. coconut oil
- Salt, ground black pepper,
- 2 bay leaves & 2 Tbsp. chopped garlic
- 2 cups beef stock & 2 cups tomato paste
- 4 pounds beef tripe cut into stripes

Instructions

Put ingredients in the slow cooker. Cover, and cook on low for 9 hours.

Cauliflower, Tomato and Minced Beef

Serves 8

Ingredients - Allergies: SF, GF, DF, EF, NF

- 2 cups chopped tomatoes
- 4 cups cauliflower florets
- 2 cups chopped onions
- 2 tbsp. coconut oil
- Salt, ground black pepper and cumin to taste
- 2 bay leaves & 2 Tbsp. chopped garlic & 1 tsp. oregano
- 2 cups beef stock & 1 cup tomato paste
- 4 pounds minced beef

Instructions

Put ingredients in the slow cooker. Cover, and cook on low for 9 hours.

Kare Kare – oxtail stew

Serves 8

Ingredients - Allergies: SF, GF, DF, EF, NF

- 2 cups broccoli
- 1 cup green beans
- 2 cups chopped onions
- 2 tbsp. coconut oil
- Salt, ground black pepper and ground cumin to taste
- 2 bay leaves & 2 Tbsp. chopped garlic
- 2 cups beef stock & 2 cups tomato paste
- 4 pounds oxtail cut into 2 inch chunks

Instructions

Put ingredients in the slow cooker. Cover, and cook on low for 9 hours.

Osso Bucco with shredded veggies

Serves 8

Ingredients - Allergies: SF, GF, DF, EF, NF

- 2 cups shredded carrots
- 2 cups chopped leeks
- 2 cups chopped celery
- Salt, ground black pepper to taste
- 2 bay leaves & 2 Tbsp. chopped garlic
- 2 cups beef stock & 1 cup white wine
- 4 pounds veal osso bucco

Instructions

Mix all veggies and spices and put half at the bottom of the slow cooker dish. Put osso bucco on top, add the rest of the mix and pour liquid. Cover, and cook on low for 9 hours.

Tuscan Pork & White Beans

Serves 8

Ingredients - Allergies: SF, GF, DF, EF, NF

- 1 cup tomatoes, sliced
- 2 cups chopped onions
- 2 cups kale or spinach
- 2 cups dry navy beans
- 2 tbsp. coconut oil
- Salt, ground black pepper and ground cumin to taste
- 2 bay leaves & 2 Tbsp. chopped garlic
- 2 cups beef stock
- 2 cups water
- 4 pounds pork shoulder meat

Instructions

Put ingredients in the slow cooker. Cover, and cook on low for 9 hours.

Leeks, Mushrooms & Pork Neck Meat

Serves 8

Ingredients - Allergies: SF, GF, DF, EF, NF

- 2 cups mushrooms, sliced
- 2 cups chopped leeks
- 2 tbsp. coconut oil
- Salt, ground black pepper and ground cumin to taste
- 2 bay leaves & 2 Tbsp. chopped garlic
- 4 cups beef stock
- ¼ cup sesame seeds
- ¼ cup chopped spring onions
- 4 pounds pork neck meat

Instructions

Put all ingredients in the slow cooker except spring onions and sesame seeds. Cover, and cook on low for 9 hours. Sprinkle with chopped spring onions and sesame seeds.

Beef, Beet, Carrots & Onions

Serves 8

Ingredients - Allergies: SF, GF, DF, EF, NF

- 2 cups julienned carrots
- 2 medium beets, peeled and sliced
- 2 cups chopped onions
- 2 tbsp. coconut oil
- Salt, ground black pepper to taste
- 2 cups beef stock
- 4 pounds cubed beef
- 2 Tbsp. minced garlic.

Instructions

Put ingredients in the slow cooker. Cover, and cook on low for 8 hours.

Broccoli, Pork & Peppers

Serves 8

Ingredients - Allergies: SF, GF, DF, EF, NF

- 2 cup sliced yellow and orange peppers
- 1 cup chopped onions
- 2 tbsp. coconut oil
- Salt, ground black pepper to taste
- 1 cup beef stock
- 2 pounds pork chops
- 2 pounds pork neck
- 2 Tbsp. minced garlic.
- 2 cups broccoli florets

Instructions

Put ingredients in the slow cooker. Cover, and cook on low for 8 hours.

Haitian Chicken Broccoli

Serves 8

Ingredients - Allergies: SF, GF, DF, EF, NF

- 2 cup broccoli florets
- 2 cups chopped onions
- 2 tbsp. coconut oil
- Salt, ground black pepper to taste
- 3 cups chicken stock
- 4 pounds cubed chicken meat
- 1 tsp. dried red pepper flakes (to taste).
- 4 whole cloves (discard after cooking)
- 2 Tbsp. minced garlic
- 1 Tbsp. apple vinegar

Instructions

Put ingredients in the slow cooker. Cover, and cook on low for 8 hours.

Leeks, Cauliflower, Chicken & Carrot

Serves 8

Ingredients - Allergies: SF, GF, DF, EF, NF

- 3 cups sliced leeks
- 2 cups carrot
- 2 tbsp. coconut oil
- Salt, ground black pepper to taste
- 2 cups chicken stock
- 4 pounds cubed chicken meat
- 2 Tbsp. minced ginger & 2 Tbsp. minced garlic.
- 2 sticks celery, chopped

Instructions

Put ingredients in the slow cooker. Cover, and cook on low for 8 hours.

Okra & Pork Stew

Serves 8

Ingredients - Allergies: SF, GF, DF, EF, NF

- 3 cups sliced okra
- 2 cups chopped onions
- 2 tbsp. coconut oil
- Salt, ground black pepper to taste
- 2 cups beef stock
- 4 pounds pork neck meat
- 5 cloves garlic, halved lengthwise
- 2 sticks celery, chopped

Instructions

Put ingredients in the slow cooker. Cover, and cook on low for 8 hours.

Chicken, Black Beans and Cauliflower

Serves 8

Ingredients - Allergies: SF, GF, DF, EF, NF

- 2 cups cauliflower
- 1 cup black beans
- 2 cups chopped onions & 3 carrots - chopped
- 2 tbsp. coconut oil
- Salt, ground black pepper to taste
- 3 cups chicken stock
- 4 pounds dark chicken meat
- 2 Tbsp. minced garlic & 1 tsp. ground cumin

Instructions

Put ingredients in the slow cooker. Cover, and cook on low for 8 hours.

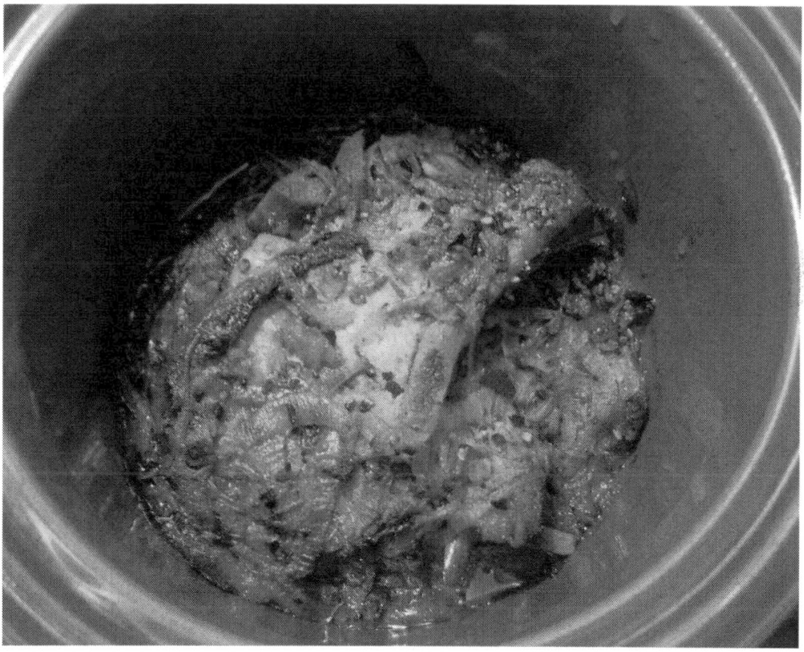

Celery, Carrots & Cauliflower Pork

Serves 8

Ingredients - Allergies: SF, GF, DF, EF, NF

- 2 cup sliced celery
- 2 cups chopped onions
- 2 tbsp. coconut oil
- Salt, ground black pepper to taste
- 2 cups beef stock
- 4 pounds cubed pork meat
- 2 cups chopped carrots
- 2 cups chopped cauliflower
- 2 Tbsp. minced garlic & 3-4 bay leaves (discard after cooking).

Instructions

Put ingredients in the slow cooker. Cover, and cook on low for 8 hours.

Slow Cooked Carnitas

Serves 8

Ingredients - Allergies: SF, GF, DF, EF, NF

- 2 cups chopped onions
- 2 tbsp. coconut oil
- Salt, ground black pepper to taste
- 2 pounds pork shoulder
- 2 pounds pork neck
- 1 Jalapeno pepper, chopped (to taste).
- 2 Tbsp. minced garlic.
- 1 Tbsp. ground cumin.

Instructions

Put ingredients in the slow cooker. Cover, and cook on low for 8 hours.

Beef & Apple

Serves 8

Ingredients - Allergies: SF, GF, DF, EF, NF

- 2 cups chopped carrots
- 2 cups chopped onions
- 2 tbsp. coconut oil
- Salt, ground black pepper to taste
- 2 cups beef stock mixed with 4 Tbsp. almond flour
- 4 pounds cubed beef
- 1 lime - juice.
- 2 Tbsp. minced garlic.
- 6 large apples, cored and cut in 8 pieces

Instructions

Put ingredients in the slow cooker. Cover, and cook on low for 8 hours.

Bigos- Polish Pork, Venison & Cabbage Stew

Serves 8

Ingredients - Allergies: SF, GF, DF, EF, NF

- 1 cup chopped onions
- 2 tbsp. coconut oil
- Salt, ground black pepper to taste
- 2 pound pork shoulder meat, cubed
- 2 pounds venison meat, cubed
- 3 cups shredded cabbage
- 2 Tbsp. minced garlic
- 1 Tbsp. ground paprika

Instructions

Put ingredients in the slow cooker. Cover, and cook on low for 8 hours.

Cumin Lamb

Serves 8

Ingredients - Allergies: SF, GF, DF, EF, NF

- 2 cups chopped onions
- 2 tbsp. coconut oil
- Salt, ground black pepper to taste
- 4 pounds lamb meat, cubed
- 1 cup parsley
- 1 cup sesame seeds
- 2 Tbsp. minced garlic
- 3 Tbsp. ground cumin

Instructions

Put ingredients in the slow cooker. Cover, and cook on low for 8 hours.

Mexican Lamb Chili

Serves 6

Ingredients - Allergies: SF, GF, DF, EF, NF

- 2 tbsp. coconut oil
- 2 onions, chopped
- 3 cloves garlic, minced
- 3 pounds cubed lamb meat
- 1 cup corn
- 1 cup tomato paste
- 2 cups beef broth
- 2 tbsp. cumin seeds
- 1 tsp. ground cayenne pepper
- 1 tsp. ground coriander
- 1 tsp. salt
- 3 cups cooked kidney beans
- 2-3 fresh hot chili peppers, chopped

Instructions

Put ingredients in the slow cooker. Cover, and cook on low for 8 hours.

Moroccan Lamb, Tomato Sauce & Green Peppers Stew

Serves 8

Ingredients - Allergies: SF, GF, DF, EF, NF

- 2 cups chopped onions
- 2 tbsp. coconut oil
- Salt, ground black pepper to taste
- 4 pounds lamb meat, cubed
- 2 cups tomato paste
- 3 cups green peppers
- 2 Tbsp. minced garlic.
- 2 Tbsp. ground cumin.

Instructions

Put ingredients in the slow cooker. Cover, and cook on low for 8 hours.

Pork, Mushrooms & Herbs Stew

Serves 8

Ingredients - Allergies: SF, GF, DF, EF, NF

- 2 cups chopped onions
- 2 tbsp. coconut oil
- Salt, ground black pepper to taste
- 4 pounds pork shoulder
- 3 cups sliced mushrooms
- 1/2 cup each parsley, cilantro and dill
- 2 Tbsp. minced garlic.

Instructions

Put ingredients in the slow cooker. Cover, and cook on low for 8 hours.

Chicken Green Curry

Serves 8

Ingredients - Allergies: SF, GF, DF, EF, NF

- 1 cup chopped onions
- 1 cup coconut milk
- 1 lime - juice & 1 cup chicken broth
- 1 cup chopped cilantro & 3 cloves garlic.
- 4 pounds chicken meat
- 2 cups sliced veggies (green beans and green peppers)
- 2 Tbsp. curry paste
- 4 Tbsp. fish sauce

Instructions

Blend lime, onions, curry paste, cilantro and spices. Put chicken and other ingredients in the slow cooker and pour blended ingredients over. Cover, and cook on low for 8 hours. Decorate with fresh basil leaves.

Two Beans Chili

Serves 8

Ingredients - Allergies: SF, GF, DF, EF, NF

- 2 tbsp. coconut oil
- 2 onions, chopped
- 3 cloves garlic, minced
- 1 pound ground beef
- 3/4 pound beef sirloin, cubed
- 2 cups diced tomatoes
- 1 cup strong brewed coffee
- 1 cup tomato paste
- 2 cups beef broth
- 1 tbsp. cumin seeds
- 1 tsp. dried oregano
- 1 tsp. ground cayenne pepper
- 1 tsp. ground coriander
- 1 tsp. salt
- 3 cups cooked kidney beans
- 3 cups cooked navy beans
- 4 fresh hot chili peppers, chopped

Instructions

Put ingredients in the slow cooker. Cover, and cook on low for 4 hours.

Chicken & Artichoke Hearts

Serves 8

Ingredients - Allergies: SF, GF, DF, EF, NF

- 2 cups chopped onions
- 2 tbsp. coconut oil
- Salt, ground black pepper to taste
- 4 pounds chicken meat
- 2 cups chopped carrots.
- 8 Artichokes, tops sliced, trimmed
- 1 Tbsp. ground cumin.
- 1 cup chicken broth

Instructions

Put ingredients in the slow cooker. Cover, and cook on low for 8 hours.

Green Peppers, Chicken and Green Onions

Serves 8

Ingredients - Allergies: SF, GF, DF, EF, NF

- 2 cups chopped green onions
- 2 tbsp. coconut oil
- Salt, ground black pepper to taste
- 4 pounds chopped chicken meat
- 2 cups sliced green peppers
- 2 Tbsp. minced garlic.
- 1 Tbsp. ground cumin.

Instructions

Put ingredients in the slow cooker. Cover, and cook on low for 8 hours.

Black Bean Chicken Chili

Serves 8

Ingredients - Allergies: SF, GF, DF, EF, NF

- 2 tbsp. coconut oil
- 2 onions, chopped
- 3 cloves garlic, minced
- 2 pounds cubed chicken meat
- 2 cups diced red and yellow peppers
- 2 cups sliced celery
- 1 cup tomato paste
- 2 cups chicken broth
- 1 tbsp. cumin seeds
- 1 tsp. dried oregano
- 1 tsp. ground cayenne pepper
- 1 tsp. ground coriander
- 1 tsp. salt
- 2 cups black beans
- 4 fresh hot chili peppers, chopped

Instructions

Put ingredients in the slow cooker. Cover, and cook on low for 8 hours.

Stir Fries

Pork and Bok Choy / Celery Stir Fry

Serves 1 - Allergies: SF, GF, DF, EF, NF

5 oz. Lean Pork Tenderloin and Bok Choy / Celery stir fry. Use as much veggies as you want or replace Bok Choy with Kale. Season with fish sauce.

Nutrition Facts

Serving Size 574 g

Amount Per Serving	
Calories 316	Calories from Fat 39
	% Daily Value*
Total Fat 4.3g	**7%**
Saturated Fat 1.1g	**6%**
Trans Fat 0.0g	
Cholesterol 82mg	**27%**
Sodium 1156mg	**48%**
Potassium 1314mg	**38%**
Total Carbohydrates 34.6g	**12%**
Dietary Fiber 8.8g	**35%**
Sugars 8.8g	
Protein 34.5g	
Vitamin A 33% •	Vitamin C 81%
Calcium 9% •	Iron 30%
Nutrition Grade A	
* Based on a 2000 calorie diet	

Lemon Chicken Stir Fry

Serves 3-4

Ingredients - Allergies: SF, GF, DF, EF, NF

- 1 lemon
- 1/2 cup chicken broth
- 3 tbsp. fish sauce
- 2 teaspoons arrowroot flour
- 1 tbsp. coconut oil
- 1 pound boneless, skinless cubed chicken breasts
- 10 ounces mushrooms, halved or quartered
- 2 cups snow peas, stems and strings removed
- 1 bunch scallions, cut into 1-inch pieces, white and green parts divided
- 1 tbsp. chopped garlic

Instructions

Grate 1 tsp. lemon zest. Juice the lemon and mix 3 tbsp. of the juice with broth, fish sauce and arrowroot flour in a small bowl.

Heat oil in a skillet over high heat. Add chicken and cook, stirring occasionally, until just cooked through. Transfer to a plate. Add mushrooms to the pan and cook until the mushrooms are tender. Add snow peas, garlic, scallion whites and the lemon zest. Cook, stirring, around 30 seconds. Add the broth to the pan and cook, stirring, 2 to 3 minutes. Add scallion greens and the chicken and any accumulated juices and stir.

Pan seared Brussels sprouts

Serves 2

Ingredients - Allergies: SF, GF, DF, EF, NF

- 6 oz. cubed pork
- 2 tbsp. coconut oil
- 1 pound Brussels sprouts, halved
- 1/2 large onion, chopped
- Salt and ground black pepper

Instructions

Cook pork in a skillet over high heat. Remove to a plate and chop. In same pan with pork fat, add coconut oil over high heat. Add onions and Brussels sprouts and cook, stirring occasionally, until sprouts are golden brown. Season with salt and pepper, to taste, and put pork back into pan. Serve immediately.

Beef and Broccoli Stir Fry

Serves 1 - Allergies: SF, GF, DF, EF, NF

- 5oz. of lean Beef and 1 cup broccoli stir fry. Use as much broccoli as you want or replace Broccoli with Kale.

Nutrition Facts

Serving Size 251 g

Amount Per Serving	
Calories 342	Calories from Fat 124
	% Daily Value*
Total Fat 13.8g	**21%**
Saturated Fat 4.0g	**20%**
Trans Fat 0.0g	
Cholesterol 127mg	**42%**
Sodium 1024mg	**43%**
Potassium 884mg	**25%**
Total Carbohydrates 7.0g	**2%**
Dietary Fiber 2.4g	**10%**
Sugars 1.7g	
Protein 46.5g	
Vitamin A 11% •	Vitamin C 131%
Calcium 5% •	Iron 154%
Nutrition Grade A-	

* Based on a 2000 calorie diet

Shrimp with Snow Peas

Serves 4.

Ingredients - Allergies: SF, GF, DF, EF, NF

Marinade

- 2 teaspoons arrowroot flour
- 1 Tbsp wine
- 1/2 tsp. salt

Stir Fry

- 1 pound shrimp, peeled and deveined
- 2 Tbsp coconut oil
- 1 Tbsp minced ginger
- 3 garlic cloves, sliced thinly
- 1/2 pound snow peas, strings removed
- 2 teaspoons fish sauce
- 1/4 cup chicken broth
- 4 green onions, white and light green parts, sliced diagonally
- 2 teaspoons dark roasted sesame oil

Instructions

Mix all the ingredients for the marinade in a bowl and then add the shrimp. Mix to coat. Let it marinade 15 minutes while you prepare the peas, ginger, and garlic.

Add the coconut oil in the wok and let it get hot. Add the garlic and combine it with ginger. Stir-fry for about 30 seconds.

Add the marinade to the wok, add the snow peas, fish sauce and chicken broth. Stir-fry until the shrimp turns pink. Add the green onions and stir-fry for one more minute. Turn off the heat and add the sesame oil. Toss once more and serve with steamed brown rice or soba gluten free noodles.

Pork and Green Beans Stir Fry

Serves 1 - Allergies: SF, GF, DF, EF, NF

- 6oz. of lean Pork
- 1 cup of Green Beans, snapped in half. Use as much veggies as you want or replace Green beans with Kale.
- 1 garlic clove, chopped
- 1/2 inch of peeled and chopped ginger
- Season with fish sauce.

Nutrition Facts	
Serving Size 285 g	
Amount Per Serving	
Calories 317	Calories from Fat 97
	% Daily Value*
Total Fat 10.8g	17%
Saturated Fat 2.7g	14%
Trans Fat 0.1g	
Cholesterol 124mg	41%
Sodium 104mg	4%
Potassium 946mg	27%
Total Carbohydrates 7.8g	3%
Dietary Fiber 3.7g	15%
Sugars 1.5g	
Protein 46.5g	
Vitamin A 15% •	Vitamin C 30%
Calcium 5% •	Iron 17%
Nutrition Grade A	
* Based on a 2000 calorie diet	

Cashew chicken

Serves 4

Ingredients - Allergies: SF, GF, DF, EF, NF

- 1 bunch scallions
- 1 pound skinless boneless chicken thighs
- 1/2 tsp. salt
- 1/4 tsp. black pepper
- 3 tbsp. coconut oil
- 1 red bell pepper and 1 stalk of celery, chopped
- 4 garlic cloves, finely chopped
- 1 1/2 tbsp. finely chopped peeled fresh ginger
- 1/4 tsp. dried hot red-pepper flakes
- 3/4 cup chicken broth
- 1 1/2 tbsp. fish sauce
- 1 1/2 teaspoons arrowroot flour
- 1/2 cup salted roasted whole cashews

Instructions

Chop scallions and separate green and white parts. Pat chicken dry and cut into 3/4-inch pieces and season with salt and pepper. Heat a wok or a skillet over high heat. Add oil and then stir-fry chicken until cooked through, 3 to 4 minutes. Transfer to a plate. Add garlic, bell pepper, celery, ginger, red-pepper flakes, and scallion whites to wok and stir-fry until peppers are just tender, 4 to 5 minutes.

Mix together broth, fish sauce and arrowroot flour, then stir into vegetables in wok. Reduce heat and simmer, stirring occasionally, until thickened. Stir in cashews, scallion greens, and chicken along with any juices.

Chinese Celery, Mushrooms & Fish Stir Fry

Serves 2

Ingredients - Allergies: SF, GF, DF, EF

- 1/2 pound fish fillets
- 1 cup Chinese Celery
- 1 cup Mushrooms sliced in half
- 1/2 cup peppers sliced diagonally
- 1 Tsp. oil

Instructions

Marinade fish in a Superfoods marinade. Stir fry drained fish in coconut oil for few minutes, add all vegetables and stir fry for 2 more minutes. Add the rest of the marinade and stir fry for a minute. Serve with brown rice or quinoa.

Pork, Green Pepper and Tomato Stir Fry

Serves 2

Ingredients - Allergies: SF, GF, DF, EF

- 1/2 pound cubed pork
- 1 cup Green Peppers
- 1/2 cup sliced Tomatoes
- 1 tsp. ground black pepper
- 1 Tsp. oil

Instructions

Marinade pork in a Superfoods marinade. Stir fry drained pork in coconut oil for few minutes, add all vegetables and stir fry for 2 more minutes. Add the rest of the marinade and stir fry for a minute. Serve with brown rice or quinoa.

Pork, Red & Green Peppers, Onion & Carrots Stir Fry

Serves 2

Ingredients - Allergies: SF, GF, DF, EF

- 1/2 pound pork
- 1/2 cup chopped Red Peppers
- 1/2 cup chopped Green Peppers
- 1/2 cup sliced onion
- 1/2 cup sliced carrots
- 1 Tsp. oil

Instructions

Marinade pork in a Superfoods marinade. Stir fry drained pork in coconut oil for few minutes, add all vegetables and stir fry for 2 more minutes. Add the rest of the marinade and stir fry for a minute. Serve with brown rice or quinoa.

Chicken, Carrots & Snow Peas Stir Fry

Serves 2

Ingredients - Allergies: SF, GF, DF, EF

- 1/2 pound chicken
- 1 cup Carrots
- 1 cup Snow Peas
- 1 Tsp. oil

Instructions

Marinade chicken in a Superfoods marinade. Stir fry drained chicken in coconut oil for few minutes, add all vegetables and stir fry for 2 more minutes. Add the rest of the marinade and stir fry for a minute. Serve with brown rice or quinoa.

Beef, Green beans, Broccoli & Carrot Stir Fry

Serves 2

Ingredients - Allergies: SF, GF, DF, EF

- 1/2 pound beef
- 1/2 cup chopped Broccoli
- 1/2 cup chopped Green beans
- 1/2 cup sliced carrots
- 1/2 cup Baby Corn
- 1 Tsp. oil

Instructions

Marinade beef in a Superfoods marinade. Stir fry drained beef in coconut oil for few minutes, add all vegetables and stir fry for 2 more minutes. Add the rest of the marinade and stir fry for a minute. Serve with brown rice or quinoa.

Pork, Onion & Bok Choy Stir Fry

Serves 2

Ingredients - Allergies: SF, GF, DF, EF

- 1/2 pound pork
- 1/2 cup sliced onions
- 1 cup sliced Bok Choy
- 1/2 cup sliced Chinese Celery
- 1 Tsp. oil

Instructions

Marinade pork in a Superfoods marinade. Stir fry drained pork in coconut oil for few minutes, add all vegetables and stir fry for 2 more minutes. Add the rest of the marinade and stir fry for a minute. Serve with brown rice or quinoa.

Chicken, Red Peppers & Bok Choy Stir Fry

Serves 2

Ingredients - Allergies: SF, GF, DF, EF

- 1/2 pound chicken
- 1/2 cup sliced onions
- 1 cup sliced Bok Choy
- 1/2 cup sliced Red Peppers
- 1 Tsp. oil

Instructions

Marinade chicken in a Superfoods marinade. Stir fry drained chicken in coconut oil for few minutes, add all vegetables and stir fry for 2 more minutes. Add the rest of the marinade and stir fry for a minute. Serve with brown rice or quinoa.

Cauliflower & Shiitake Stir Fry

Serves 2

Ingredients - Allergies: SF, GF, DF, EF

- 2 cups Cauliflower
- 1 cup sliced Shiitake mushrooms
- 1/2 cup sliced Green beans
- 1/2 cup sliced Broccoli
- 1/2 cup sliced carrot
- 1 Tsp. Coconut oil

Instructions

Stir fry cauliflower and broccoli in coconut oil for few minutes, add carrots and green beans and stir fry for 2 more minutes. Add the mushrooms and stir fry for 3 minutes more. Serve with brown rice or quinoa.

Pork, Cabbage & Bok Choy Stir Fry

Serves 2

Ingredients - Allergies: SF, GF, DF, EF

- 1/2 pound cubed pork
- 1 cup sliced Chinese cabbage
- 1/2 cup sliced bok choy
- 1/2 cup sliced red peppers
- 1 Tsp. oil

Instructions

Marinade pork in a Superfoods marinade. Stir fry drained pork in coconut oil for few minutes, add all vegetables and stir fry for 2 more minutes. Add the rest of the marinade and stir fry for a minute. Serve with brown rice or quinoa.

Chicken & Chinese Celery Stir Fry

Serves 2

Ingredients - Allergies: SF, GF, DF, EF

- 1/2 pound chicken
- 2 cups sliced Chinese Celery
- 1 Tsp. oil

Instructions

Marinade chicken in a Superfoods marinade. Stir fry drained chicken in coconut oil for few minutes, add Chinese celery and stir fry for 2 more minutes. Add the rest of the marinade and stir fry for a minute. Serve with brown rice or quinoa.

Meats

Baked Chicken Breast with Fresh Basil

Serves 10

Ingredients - Allergies: SF, GF, EF, NF

- 10 boneless skinless chicken breast
- 3/4 cup low-fat yogurt
- 1/2 cup chopped basil
- 2 tsp. arrowroot flour
- 1 cup oatmeal coarsely ground

Instructions

Arrange chicken in a baking dish. Combine basil, yogurt and arrowroot flour; mix well and spread over chicken.

Mix oatmeal with salt and pepper to taste and sprinkle over chicken.

Bake chicken in 375 degrees in the oven for half an hour. Makes 10 servings.

Roast Chicken with Rosemary

Serves 6-8

- 1 (3 pound) whole chicken, rinsed, skinned
- salt and pepper to taste
- 1 onion, quartered
- 1/4 cup chopped rosemary

Instructions - Allergies: SF, GF, DF, EF, NF

Heat the oven to 350F. Sprinkle salt and pepper on meat. Stuff with the onion and rosemary. Place in a baking dish and bake in the preheated oven until chicken is cooked through. Depending on the size of the bird, cooking time will vary.

Carne Asada

Serves 4-6 - Allergies: SF, GF, DF, EF, NF

Marinade:

Mix together the garlic, jalapeno, cilantro, salt, and pepper to make a paste. Put the paste in a container. Add the oil, lime juice and orange juice. Shake it up to combine. Use as a marinade for beef or as a table condiment.

Instructions

Put the flank steak in a baking dish and pour the marinade over it. Refrigerate up to 8 hours.
Take the steak out of the marinade and season it on both sides with salt and pepper. Grill (or broil) the steak for 7 to 10 minutes per side, turning once, until medium-rare. Put the steak on a cutting board and allow the juices to settle (5 minutes). Thinly slice the steak across the grain.

Meatballs

Baked Beef Meatballs

This amount is for 4 servings. Adjust for 2 if you want, eat one serving, freeze one or prepare it as is for 4 servings and then freeze 3/4 for some tasty casserole recipes like "Beef Meatballs Casserole with Green Beans" or with "Beef Meatballs Casserole with Broccoli".

Allergies: SF, GF, NF

- 1 pound lean ground beef
- 2 tbsp. minced onion
- 1/2 tsp. minced garlic
- 1 tsp. parmesan cheese
- 2 eggs
- 1/2 tsp. salt
- 1/4 tsp. pepper

Mix all of the ingredients in a large bowl using your fingers. Mix until the meat no long feels slimy from the eggs. Shape in small egg size meatballs. Place on a baking sheet. Bake at 375F for 20-25 minutes until the meatballs are cooked through. Serve with large Fiber Loaded salad

Nutrition Facts

Serving Size 149 g

Amount Per Serving	
Calories 268	Calories from Fat 97
	% Daily Value*
Total Fat 10.8g	**17%**
Saturated Fat 4.3g	**22%**
Trans Fat 0.0g	
Cholesterol 188mg	**63%**
Sodium 461mg	**19%**
Potassium 497mg	**14%**
Total Carbohydrates 1.1g	**0%**
Protein 39.5g	
Vitamin A 3% •	Vitamin C 1%
Calcium 8% •	Iron 121%
Nutrition Grade B	

* Based on a 2000 calorie diet

with Italian Dressing.

Middle Eastern Meatballs

Makes about 20 meatballs - Allergies: SF, GF, DF, EF, NF

Ingredients

- Ground lamb or beef, or a mixture of the two -- 2 pounds
- Onion, minced -- 1
- Fresh parsley or mint, finely chopped -- 1/2 bunch
- Ground cumin -- 1 tbsp.
- Cinnamon -- 2 teaspoons
- Allspice (optional) -- 1 tsp.
- Salt and pepper -- to season
- coconut oil -- 1/4 cup

Instructions

Place the ground beef or lamb, onion, herbs, spices, salt and pepper in a bowl and knead well. Chill for 1-2 hours and let the flavors mingle. Form the meat into patties or balls the size of a small egg.

Bake in the oven on 350F. Serve with brown rice with tzatziki sauce.

Variations

Experiment with different seasonings--coriander, cayenne, sesame seeds.

Fish

Cioppino

Serves 6

Ingredients - Allergies: SF, GF, DF, EF, NF

- 3/4 cup coconut oil
- 2 onions, chopped
- 2 cloves garlic, minced
- 1 bunch fresh parsley, chopped
- 1,5 cups stewed tomatoes
- 1,5 cups chicken broth
- 2 bay leaves
- 1 tbsp. dried basil
- 1/2 tsp. dried thyme
- 1/2 tsp. dried oregano
- 1 cup water
- 1-1/2 cups white wine
- 1-1/2 pounds peeled and deveined large shrimp
- 1-1/2 pounds bay scallops
- 18 small clams
- 18 cleaned and debearded mussels
- 1-1/2 cups crabmeat
- 1-1/2 pounds cod fillets, cubed

Instructions

Over medium heat melt coconut oil in a large stockpot and add onions, parsley and garlic. Cook slowly, stirring occasionally until

onions are soft. Add tomatoes to the pot. Add chicken broth, oregano, bay leaves, basil, thyme, water and wine. Mix well. Cover and simmer 30 minutes.
Stir in the shrimp, scallops, clams, mussels and crabmeat. Stir in fish. Bring to boil. Lower heat, cover and simmer until clams open.

Flounder with Orange Coconut Oil

Serves 6

Ingredients - Allergies: SF, GF, DF, EF, NF

- 31/2 lbs. flounder
- 3 tbsp. white wine
- 3 tbsp. lemon juice
- 3 tbsp. coconut oil
- 3 tbsp. parsley
- 1 tsp. black pepper
- 2 tbsp. orange zest
- 1/2 tsp. salt
- 1/2 cup chopped scallions

Instructions

Preheat oven to 325F. Sprinkle fish with pepper and salt.
Place fish in the baking dish. Sprinkle orange zest on top of the fish. Melt remaining coconut oil and add the parsley and scallions to the coconut oil and pour over flounder. Then add in the white wine.
Place in oven and bake for 15 minutes. Serve fish with extra juice on a side.

Grilled Salmon

Serves 4

Ingredients - Allergies: SF, GF, DF, EF, NF

- 4 (4 ounce) filets salmon
- 1/4 cup coconut oil
- 2 tbsp. fish sauce
- 2 tbsp. lemon juice
- 2 tbsp. thinly sliced green onion
- 1 clove garlic, minced & 3/4 tsp. ground ginger
- 1/2 tsp. crushed red pepper flakes
- 1/2 tsp. sesame oil
- 1/8 tsp. salt

Instructions

Whisk together coconut oil, fish sauce, garlic, ginger, red chili flakes, lemon juice, green onions, sesame oil, and salt. Put fish in a glass dish, and pour marinade over. Cover and refrigerate for 4 hours.

Preheat grill. Place salmon on grill. Grill until fish becomes tender. Turn halfway during cooking.

Crab Cakes

Serves 6-8

Ingredients - Allergies: SF, GF, DF, NF

- 3 lbs. crabmeat
- 3 beaten eggs
- 3 cups flax seeds meal
- 3 tbsp. mustard
- 2 tbsp. grated horseradish
- 1/2 cup coconut oil
- 1 tsp. lemon rind
- 3 tbsp. lemon juice
- 2 tbsp. parsley
- 1/2 tsp. cayenne pepper
- 2 tsp. fish sauce

Instructions

In medium bowl combine all ingredients except oil. Shape in to smallish hamburgers. In fry pan heat oil and cook patties for 3-4 minutes on each side or until golden brown. Optionally, bake them in the oven.

Serve as appetizers or as main course with large fiber salad.

Superfoods Casseroles

Some recipes are for 1 person, adjust for 2 or more

Broccoli Chicken Casserole

Serves 1

Ingredients - Allergies: SF, GF, NF

- 1 cup broccoli florets
- 6 oz. skinless, boneless cubed chicken (or turkey)
- 1 tsp of flax seeds meal
- Salt, pepper
- 1 egg - beaten
- Half a cup of Yogurt Dressing (or coconut milk, if you don't like the sourish tang)
- 1/4 cup of chicken broth
- 2 tbsp of grated low-fat cheddar cheese

Heat the oven to 400°. Put broccoli and chicken in a pot, pour water over so they're barely covered, bring to boil and cook for 5 minutes.

Combine broth, flax, salt and pepper in a pan and mix. Bring to a boil over high heat and cook 1 minute, stirring constantly. Remove from heat. Add yogurt dressing, beaten egg and half of the cheese, stirring until well combined. Add sauce to broccoli mixture; and stir gently until combined.

Put mixture in a small casserole dish oiled with some coconut oil. Put remaining cheese on top, sprinkle. Bake at 400° for 50 minutes or until mixture bubbles at the edges and cheese begins to brown. Remove from oven and let cool for 5 minutes.

Chicken & Mushrooms Casserole

Serves 2

Ingredients - Allergies: SF, GF, DF, EF, NF

- 1 large onion, chopped
- 3 cups sliced mushrooms
- 2 tbsp. coconut oil
- 1/2 tsp. salt
- 1/4 tsp. ground black pepper
- 1/2 tsp. minced garlic
- 2 large chicken breast pieces with skin on

Instructions

Oil casserole dish with oil, put chicken pieces in. Mix onion, salt, pepper, mushrooms and garlic and put over chicken. Cover and bake for 1 ½ hours on 400F.

Pork & Red Peppers Casserole

Serves 8

Ingredients - Allergies: SF, GF, NF

- 1 cup chopped onions
- 2 cups sliced Red Peppers
- 4 pounds cubed pork
- 1 cup "healthy casserole sauce"

Instructions

Put all ingredients in the casserole dish, pour sauce on top, cover and bake for 2 hours on 400F. Garnish with parsley.

Chicken, Carrot and Cherry Tomatoes Casserole

Serves 8

Ingredients - Allergies: SF, GF, DF, EF, NF

- 1 cup chopped carrots
- 1 cup chopped onions
- 2 tbsp. coconut oil
- 1-1/2 cups yellow peppers
- 1/2 tsp. salt
- 1/4 tsp. ground black pepper
- 1/2 tsp. minced garlic
- 4 pounds cubed chicken
- 1/2 cups chopped parsley

Instructions

Put all ingredients in the casserole dish, cover and bake for 2 hours on 400F.

Chicken, Carrot and Onions Italian Casserole

Serves 6

Ingredients - Allergies: SF, GF, DF, EF, NF

- 1 cup chopped carrots
- 1 cup chopped onions
- 2 tbsp. coconut oil
- 1 cup sliced mushrooms
- 1/2 tsp. salt
- 1/4 tsp. ground black pepper
- 1/2 tsp. minced garlic
- 1 tsp. fresh rosemary
- 4 pounds chicken with skin on

Instructions

Put all ingredients in the casserole dish, cover and bake for 2 hours on 400F.

Red Peppers, Zucchini and Eggplant Casserole

Serves 8

Ingredients - Allergies: SF, GF, DF, EF, NF

- 1 chopped carrots
- 1 cup chopped onions
- 1 - 1/2 cup sliced red peppers
- 2 tbsp. coconut oil
- 1 cup sliced zucchini
- 1/2 tsp. salt
- 1/4 tsp. ground black pepper
- 1/2 tsp. minced garlic
- 1/2 tsp. oregano
- 2 pounds sliced eggplant

Instructions

Put all ingredients in the casserole dish, cover and bake for 2 hours on 400F.

Osso Bucco Casserole

Serves 6-8

Ingredients - Allergies: SF, GF, DF, EF, NF

- 1-1/2 cups sliced mushrooms
- 1 1.2 cups chopped onions
- 2 tbsp. coconut oil
- 1 cup beef stock
- 1/2 tsp. salt
- 1/4 tsp. ground black pepper
- 1 tsp. minced garlic
- 1 tsp. chopped parsley
- 4 pounds osso bucco

Instructions

Put all ingredients in the casserole dish, cover and bake for 2 hours on 400F. Onions and mushrooms should be almost melted and turned into a sauce after 2 hours. Garnish with chopped parsley.

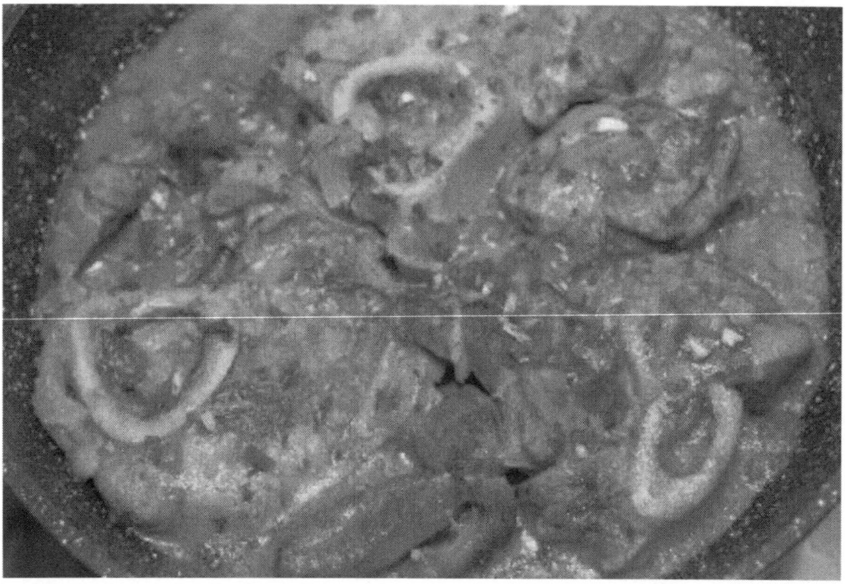

Chicken, Olives & Garlic Casserole

Serves 8

Ingredients - Allergies: SF, GF, DF, EF, NF

- 1 cup chopped onions
- 2 tbsp. coconut oil
- 1 cup Kalamata olives
- 1/4 tsp. ground black pepper
- 1 head garlic, sliced across (bake separately for 45 minutes)
- 1 Tbsp. fresh rosemary
- 4 pounds chicken pieces (dark meat) with skin on

Instructions

Put chicken, onions and olives in the casserole dish, season, cover and bake for 2 hours on 400F. Serve with baked garlic.

Shrimp, Tomato Paste and Red Peppers Casserole

Serves 4

Ingredients - Allergies: SF, GF, DF, EF, NF

- 1/2 cups chopped carrots
- 1 cup chopped red peppers
- 1/2 cup chopped onions
- 2 tbsp. coconut oil
- 2 cups tomato paste - see recipe at the beginning
- 1/2 tsp. salt
- 1/4 tsp. ground black pepper
- 1 tsp. minced garlic
- 2 pounds shrimp

Instructions

Put all ingredients in the casserole dish, cover and bake for 2 hours on 400F.

Pork Chop Casserole

Serves 1

Ingredients - Allergies: SF, GF, DF, EF, NF

- 3 cups vegetable broth
- 5 ounce mushrooms
- salt and pepper to taste
- 6 (3/4 inch) thick pork chops

Instructions

Heat oven to 350F. Pour broth into a baking dish. Add mushrooms and mix. Salt and pepper to taste. Add pork chops in a single layer on that mixture and push them down into mixture and make sure they are covered with it.
Cover baking dish with aluminum foil and bake for 1 hour.

Mushrooms Casserole

Instructions – serves 4 - Allergies: SF, GF, NF

- 3 pounds sliced mushrooms (shiitake preferably)
- 1 pound sliced leeks
- Salt and freshly ground black pepper
- 1 tbsp. chopped parsley
- 2 beaten eggs
- 1 cup of low-fat Greek yogurt
- 1/2 cup of shredded cheddar cheese, low-fat
- 1 pound cubed skinless boneless chicken (or turkey) breasts

Instructions

Heat oven to 375 degrees F. Mix beaten eggs and low-fat yogurt in a separate dish. In a casserole, place 1 layer of mushrooms, leeks and chicken cubes and season with salt, pepper, and parsley. Cover with 1/2 of a cup of eggs/yogurt mixture. Repeat process 2 more times and cover with shredded cheese. Bake until mushrooms and chicken is tender and crust is golden brown.

Chicken Eggplant Casserole

Ingredients – serves 4 - Allergies: SF, GF, NF

- 3 pounds Eggplant
- Salt and ground black pepper
- 1 tbsp. chopped parsley
- 2 beaten eggs
- 1 cup of low-fat Greek yogurt
- 1/2 cup of shredded cheddar cheese, low-fat
- 1 pound cubed skinless boneless chicken (or turkey) breasts

Instructions

Preheat oven to 375 degrees F. Mix beaten eggs and low-fat yogurt in a separate dish. In a casserole, place 1 layer of eggplant and meat cubes. Sprinkle with salt, pepper, and parsley. Cover with 1/2 of a cup of eggs/yogurt mixture. Repeat process 2 more times and cover with shredded cheese. Bake until eggplant and chicken are tender and crust is golden brown, about 20 minutes. Serve with Large Fiber Loaded salad with Italian Dressing.

Superfoods Reference Book

Unfortunately, I had to take out the whole Superfoods Reference Book out of all of my books because parts of that book are featured on my blog. I joined Kindle Direct Publishing Select program which allows me to have all my books free for 5 days every 3 months. Unfortunately, KDP Select program also means that all my books have to have unique content that is not available in any other online store or on the Internet (including my blog). I didn't want to remove parts of Superfoods Reference book that is already on my blog because I want that all people have free access to that information. I also wanted to be part of KDP Select program because that is an option to give my book for free to anyone. So, some sections of my Superfoods Reference Book can be found on my blog, under Superfoods menu on my blog. Complete Reference book is available for subscribers to my Superfoods Today Newsletter. Subscribers to my Newsletter will also get information whenever any of my books becomes free on Amazon. I will not offer any product pitches or anything similar to my subscribers, only Superfoods related information, recipes and weight loss and fitness tips. So, subscribe to my newsletter, download Superfoods Today Desserts free eBook which has complete Superfood Reference book included and have the opportunity to get all of my future books for free.

Your Free Gift

As a way of saying thanks for your purchase, I'm offering you my FREE eBook that is exclusive to my book and blog readers.

Superfoods Cookbook Book Two has over 70 Superfoods recipes and complements Superfoods Cookbook Book One and it contains Superfoods Salads, Superfoods Smoothies and Superfoods Deserts with ultra-healthy non-refined ingredients. All ingredients are 100% Superfoods.

It also contains Superfoods Reference book which is organized by Superfoods (more than 60 of them, with the list of their benefits), Superfoods spices, all vitamins, minerals and antioxidants. Superfoods Reference Book lists Superfoods that can help with 12 diseases and 9 types of cancer.

http://www.SuperfoodsToday.com/FREE

Other Books from this Author

Superfoods Today Diet is a Kindle Superfoods Diet book that gives you 4 week Superfoods Diet meal plan as well as 2 weeks maintenance meal plan and recipes for weight loss success. It is an extension of Detox book and it's written for people who want to switch to Superfoods lifestyle.

Superfoods Today Body Care is a Kindle book with over 50 Natural Recipes for beautiful skin and hair. It has body scrubs, facial masks and hair care recipes made with the best Superfoods like avocado honey, coconut, olive oil, oatmeal, yogurt, banana and Superfoods herbs like lavender, rosemary, mint, sage, hibiscus, rose.

Superfoods Today Cookbook is a Kindle book that contains over 160 Superfoods recipes created with 100% Superfoods ingredients. Most of the meals can be prepared in under 30 minutes and some are really quick ones that can be done in 10 minutes only. Each recipe combines Superfoods ingredients that deliver astonishing amounts of antioxidants, essential fatty acids (like omega-3), minerals, vitamins, and more.

Superfoods Today Smoothies is a Kindle Superfoods Smoothies book with over 70+ 100% Superfoods smoothies. Featured are Red, Purple, Green and Yellow Smoothies

Superfoods Today Salads is a Kindle book that contains over 60 Superfoods Salads recipes created with 100% Superfoods ingredients. Most of the salads can be prepared in 10 minutes and most are measured for two. Each recipe combines Superfoods ingredients that deliver astonishing amounts of antioxidants, essential fatty acids (like omega-3), minerals, vitamins, and more.

Superfoods Today Kettlebells is a Kindle Kettlebells beginner's book aimed at 30+ office workers who want to improve their health and build stronger body without fat.

Superfoods Today Red Smoothies is a Kindle Superfoods Smoothies book with more than 40 Red Smoothies.

Superfoods Today 14 Days Detox is a Kindle Superfoods Detox book that gives you 2 week Superfoods Detox meal plan and recipes for Detox success.

Superfoods Today Yellow Smoothies is a Kindle Superfoods Smoothies book with more than 40 Yellow Smoothies.

Superfoods Today Green Smoothies is a Kindle Superfoods Smoothies book with more than 35 Green Smoothies.

Superfoods Today Purple Smoothies is a Kindle Superfoods Smoothies book with more than 40 Purple Smoothies.

Superfoods Cooking For Two is a Kindle book that contains over 150 Superfoods recipes for two created with 100% Superfoods ingredients.

Nighttime Eater is a Kindle book that deals with Nighttime Eating Syndrome (NES). Don Orwell is a life-long Nighttime Eater that has lost his weight with Superfoods and engineered a solution around Nighttime Eating problem. Don still eats at night☺. Don't fight your nature, you can continue to eat at night, be binge free and maintain low weight.

Superfoods Today Smart Carbs 20 Days Detox is a Kindle Superfoods book that will teach you how to detox your body and start losing weight with Smart Carbs. The book has over 470+ pages with over 160+ 100% Superfoods recipes.

Superfoods Today Vegetarian Salads is a Kindle book that contains over 40 Superfoods Vegetarian Salads recipes created with 100% Superfoods ingredients. Most of the salads can be prepared in 10 minutes and most are measured for two.

Superfoods Today Vegan Salads is a Kindle book that contains over 30 Superfoods Vegan Salads recipes created with 100% Superfoods ingredients. Most of the salads can be prepared in 10 minutes and most are measured for two.

Superfoods Today Soups & Stews is a Kindle book that contains over 70 Superfoods Soups and Stews recipes created with 100% Superfoods ingredients.

Superfoods Desserts is a Kindle Superfoods Desserts book with more than 60 Superfoods Recipes.

Smoothies for Diabetics is a Kindle book that contains over 70 Superfoods Smoothies adjusted for diabetics.

50 Shades of Superfoods for Two is a Kindle book that contains over 150 Superfoods recipes for two created with 100% Superfoods ingredients.

50 Shades of Smoothies is a Kindle book that contains over 70 Superfoods Smoothies.

50 Shades of Superfoods Salads is a Kindle book that contains over 60 Superfoods Salads recipes created with 100% Superfoods ingredients. Most of the salads can be prepared in 10 minutes and most are measured for two. Each recipe combines Superfoods ingredients that deliver astonishing amounts of antioxidants, essential fatty acids (like omega-3), minerals, vitamins, and more.

Superfoods Vegan Desserts is a Kindle Vegan Dessert book with 100% Vegan Superfoods Recipes.

***Desserts* for Two** is a Kindle Superfoods Desserts book with more than 40 Superfoods Desserts Recipes for two.

Superfoods Paleo Cookbook is a Kindle Paleo book with more than 150 100% Superfoods Paleo Recipes.

Superfoods Breakfasts is a Kindle Superfoods book with more than 40 100% Superfoods Breakfasts Recipes.

Superfoods Dump Dinners is a Kindle Superfoods book with Superfoods Dump Dinners Recipes.

Healthy Desserts is a Kindle Desserts book with more than 50 100% Superfoods Healthy Desserts Recipes.

Superfoods Salads in a Jar is a Kindle Salads in a Jar book with more than 35 100% Superfoods Salads Recipes.

Smoothies for Kids is a Kindle Smoothies book with more than 80 100% Superfoods Smoothies for Kids Recipes.

Vegan Cookbook for Beginners is a Kindle Vegan book with more than 75 100% Superfoods Vegan Recipes.

Vegetarian Cooking for Beginners is a Kindle Vegetarian book with more than 150 100% Superfoods Paleo Recipes.

Foods for Diabetics is a Kindle book with more than 170 100% Superfoods Diabetics Recipes.

16521405R00167

Printed in Great Britain
by Amazon